T0147121

PSYCHIC DEVELOPMENT AND MEDIUMSHIP

17 STEP-BY STEP-LESSONS AND 19 GUIDED MEDITATIONS

Karen Bernabo

BALBOA.
PRESS

A DIVISION OF HAY HOUSE

Balboa Press books may be ordered through booksellers or by contacting:

Balboa Press
A Division of Hay House
1663 Liberty Drive
Bloomington, IN 47403
www.balboapress.com.au
1 (877) 407-4847

Print information available on the last page.

ISBN: 978-1-5043-0003-2 (sc)
ISBN: 978-1-5043-0004-9 (e)

Balboa Press rev. date: 11/18/2015

To my son Daniel Davern, and to all my teachers and students who are working in the light, as well as to all my spirit guides, mentors, friends and helpers, and the Ascended masters, spiritual hierarchy, and Angelic realm.

This book is dedicated with gratitude to my husband Frank for believing in me and the work that I do with spirit and for funding the many projects that I undertake within my spiritual journey.

With Gratitude to God, the Angelic realm, Ascended Masters and all of my spirit guide friends and helpers who are always there for me, and who, I always say that I would be able to do nothing without.

Thank you to all of my students over the many years that I have been teaching that had asked me to put my teachings into books so that you could "take me home with you". You all encouraged me to believe that I had something worthwhile to share with others on a larger scale than my class room.

For eternal gratitude and heartfelt thanks for all of the weekly absent/distant healings that were done for myself and my husband Frank from Helen Shilkin. May the Angels continually bring blessings to you and your family.

Many thanks to Sarah Jollie for your continued support and friendship.

A special thank you to Wendy Lawton-Scott for all of the secretarial and editorial work with scribing all of my meditations onto the pages of this book and for your friendship.

CONTENTS

INTRODUCTION

This book has come into being through the many students that have come to my classes and saying that they would love my teachings to be in a book, to read, to understand more fully what we do in class. Also many said that they had been in other classes with other teachers who did not place any protection around the room that they were working in. I found this disturbing as I believe that once a person knows how to clear and protect not just their energies but the space they work in that it would become second nature. So, it led me to believe that maybe some people had not been taught how to do this process.

This book is a hands on work book for teachers of psychic development and Mediumship circles and for students who wish to have more knowledge of what happens in a class for them to have further studies.

For those that wish to use this book to teach and run their own classes, I would highly recommend for them to have been a student in a physical class with a good experienced teacher for guidance to develop under. It takes on average of between two and five years for a person to fully develop their Mediumship skills. So, you would want your teacher not just to have good Mediumship skills to give a good reading, but more importantly have a good basic background in psychic and spiritual knowledge. For those that wish to teach, your students will also want you to have a good knowledge base. It is also for your and everyone else's safety that you know how to see or hear or sense spirit entities so that you can tell the positive ones from the negative ones and then act accordingly.

For those of you that have the skill set required to teach, you will find this a good work book to follow as it has seventeen different class lessons with nineteen meditations. You can use each of these lessons with meditations to create a new class each week. By the time you get to the last one number seventeen, that will obviously take your weekly class seventeen weeks to complete, you can just start again at number 1. It takes time to develop each of the skills to master that each lesson offers, so your students will enjoy getting in more practise in honing their skills.

CHAPTER 1

PLANNING/CIRCLE ETIQUETTE-GROUND RULES

You can run a class with as little as two people but I prefer six people with no more than twelve students in one sitting. You will need to advertise to find students for your new class if you do not belong to a Spiritualist church, then you will need to advertise in your local paper announcing that you have a new class available.

I recommend having at least two different timeslots available, one in the day preferably within school hours and the other in the evening or on a Saturday for those that work full time through the week. I personally run classes into two hour timeslots as I feel that two hours is enough time for students to learn in without feeling overwhelmed. Classes should be run once a week at the designated time. Work out in advance if it suits you and the students to hold classes throughout the school holidays. If most of your students have young children, you may find it necessary to have your classes on hold throughout the holiday period.

You may find it useful to write a paper on class etiquette/ground rules and give it to each student on commencement of them starting classes with you. An example of what I use it as follows.

1. No alcohol consumed on the day of class.
2. No recreational drug use on day of class/preferably not at all.

3. No swearing in class.
4. Be respectful to the viewpoints and feelings of others.
5. Do not interrupt when others are giving messages.
6. Do not wear perfume in class as it interferes with receiving messages where scent is often brought in with the smell of flowers from spirit
7. Please be punctual to class as others time is as precious as yours is to you.
8. It is important to be consistently coming to class on a weekly basis for your development, and all so for having consistent energy in the group.
9. If you have a personality conflict with someone in the group, do not voice it openly in the class, but to see the teacher privately afterwards.
10. When another student asks the teacher's advice, do not answer for him/her to offer your opinion as you are not the teacher of the class and everyone needs to be respectful.

CHAPTER 2

CLEARING AND CLEANSING THE ROOM AND ENERGY PROTECTION

Room Clearing, Cleansing & Protecting:

This is useful for those of us who work as teachers and/or practitioners where we need to clear a room that we are working in before and after teaching a class or working with a client. It is also useful for when you are travelling, to clear out your motel room or the room that you will sleeping in or staying at a friend's house.

Any place that we own or that we have personal use of, such as renting a motel room, then gives us the right to do the work of clearing etc. We cannot however, go about doing this work wherever we like as it may interfere with another's free will. We need to get others permission to do their home or shop/business if we are not renting their premises or a room within it. If we fail to do so, and we just go ahead thinking that it is for their highest good, then we may incur some negative karma as a response to this!

To do the room cleansing, clearing and protection repeat the following:

I ask please for Archangel Michael to create a whirly wind that is going from the centre of the room and as it expands it is pushing out all negative and unwanted entities, energies, enemies, thought forms and influences, etheric dross, negative emotions and feelings, any type of manipulation energy and anything created by them or because of them. Also anything that has come from curses, hexes, negative spells and incantations, and anything else that goes against my higher self and/or is not for my highest good.

I ask please that all of these things be completely pushed out of the room and away from me, then removed and captured into indigo blue bubbles and either be destroyed by being cast into the divine light above or thrown into the cosmic fire, or sent back to their point of origin or whatever lower dimension it is that they come from and never to come near me or to this place again.

I ask please Archangel Michael to push out and away from my personal protective shielding another shielding to go from me expanding out to the outer edges of this room that I am in and make this shielding a trillion million times stronger than any shielding that has ever been around here before. I ask please for the same to be done with Archangel Metatrons shielding and Commander Ashtar's shielding along with any other high being from the divine golden white light that can and is willing to place their shielding around it and remain in place for at least the next 24 hours.

I now ask please for St Germain to bring your violet flame of transmutation right through this room as many times as what is needed between now and the next 24 hours.

I call on the Angels of Progression to please take any earthbound entities by the hand into the light to where they belong and, if there is any resistance, I ask please for Archangel Michael to lend his assistance to escort them into the light to ensure their full progression.

I ask please for the golden spiral of protection also to be placed completely around this room and then to be held within a golden bubble of protection that is surrounded by an indigo blue shield, which is impenetrable except to the higher forces above from the divine light.

Now I ask for a two way mirror shield of protection to be placed right around all of that, and made so that I can see perfectly clearly through it and that all of my psychic abilities are completely enhanced, including, clairvoyance, clairaudience, claircogniance and clairsentience. I ask for this to be in place where ever needed or wanted, and that no psychically prying eyes can see in unless my higher self gives permission, otherwise they just see Gods golden divine white light shining back at them.

I ask for a golden merkabah of protection to be placed completely around this room and that it is surrounded by St Germains' violet flame of transmutation going a million times faster than the speed of light. As it goes around the room it actively seeks out and transmutes all negative energies instantly into positive energies and for it to be absorbed into the nearest person that needs it the most.

I ask please now for Archangel Raphael to fill this room with as much healing energy as possible for what I personally need and all that also enter this place and is with me for their highest good.

I thank all of the higher beings for all of the help for cleansing, clearing, protecting and healing that is in place now and for at least the next 24 hours.

*If you find that following these exercises on a daily basis still does not seem to be enough to keep yourself clear of negative energies in your life and nothing seems to be going right for you, then you may be under heavy psychic attack. If this is the case, then you may need the services of two mediums with expertise in this field to guide you with the best course of action if someone has placed a hex or curse upon you. Check if at least one of them is able to easily hear the Lords of Karma. This is essential as they may give you permission to stop the person or people responsible if it has gone on for a long time and they are continually breaking universal laws by psychically attacking you.

CHAPTER 3

ASCENSION COLUMN OF LIGHT AND SETTING THE INTENTION

For this you need to ask for the higher beings to assist you in this task. Firstly, I ask for golden divine white light from the heart of God (source energy) and go right into the heart of mother earth and then go through to the highest vibrational crystal gridline and back again. I ask for this to go right through the entire property known as (insert address) and to be fully anchored on a permanent basis.

If you are renting a room to work from then you would contain it to that space only to place the ascension column of light.

You can then also ask for the pillars of light to be placed in the four corners of the property, or your home or the room/space that you work in. These also go right to the heart of source and also down into the heart of mother earth.

You can also ask for Archangel Michael and his spiritual warriors to place guards on and around each and every entry and exit point of the property/building/room/space and to make sure that nothing negative gains entry as only higher vibrational beings from the light are welcome to enter. You can also ask the same of Archangel Metatron with his spiritual warriors too and also Commander Ashtar of the Ashtar command.

Once all of this is established, I then ask for it to be strengthened every 24 hours.

CHAPTER 4

OPENING THE CIRCLE AND CLOSING THE CIRCLE

Opening the circle:

We ask for the golden circle of protection to be placed around each person and right around the room. Now see your Aura reach out to enfold each person. As I mention each of the Chakras see them open out into a beautiful spiral of colour, starting with red at the base, orange for the sacral chakra, yellow for the solar plexus, peach/apricot for the soul light, green for the heart, pink for the thymus, sky blue for the throat, indigo night sky blue for the third eye and violet for the crown at the top of the head.

Now see a shaft of brilliant white light that reaches right out into the universe and we ask first that all the guides friends and helpers pass through this white light to be with us and we ask the divine for his presence among us.

Closing the circle:

Just prior to closing I ask for all of the energy that has been built up during the class to be converted into healing energy, to be taken to all those that we ask for please, by the highest healing beings that can help. The teacher/facilitator of the group starts by asking for healing for all of their loved ones, and says thank you for two reasons. Firstly, to thank the guides for doing the work, and secondly, it lets the next person know it is their turn to place their loved ones into the healing circle.

Also if there is anyone in the group that is unwell, get the entire group to visualise them in the middle of the circle and see them looking happy, vibrant, healthy and full of energy.

The teacher/facilitator then asks for each of the students to take whatever healing they need for themselves at this time by just drawing it in from the centre of the circle.

Now, as I mention each of your chakras see them closing into a tight little bud and place a cross of white light upon each of them. Starting at the crown at the top of the head, the third eye, the throat, the thymus, the heart, the soul light, the solar plexus, the sacral chakra and the base chakra. Now bring your aura back in close around you until it forms an egg shape of colour.

Ask for Archangel Michael to be each and every one of our spirit bodyguards and to place his protective shielding around each and every one of us connecting it to divine source and filling it with divine source energy and making it a million times stronger than any protection that has been around any of us before. Ask for the same to be done with Archangel Metatrons shielding and Commander Ashtar's shielding and any other higher being in the light that would like to place their protective shielding and cloaking around each of us or any of us at all.

Follow this by the golden spiral of protection, held within a golden bubble of protection, with a shield of reflective and impenetrable except to the higher forces above of indigo blue right around that, then a two mirror shield of protection right around it, that we can each see perfectly clearly out of with all our psychic abilities enhanced, including, clairvoyance, clairaudience, clairsentient, claircogniance and spirit Mediumship, wherever needed and or wanted where no psychically prying eyes can see in, unless each of our higher selves over our selves gives permission to do so, otherwise they just see Gods healing and loving light reflected shining back at them.

I then ask that we are all placed in golden merkabers of protection, that are surrounded by Saint Germain's Violet flame of transmutation that goes a million times faster than the speed of light and keeps out all negative energy and transmutes it into positive energy, and I ask that it be absorbed into the closest person or place that needs it the most.

I ask for all this to be in place now and for at least the next 24 hours. I also ask for each and every one of us to have the highest healing given to us that is possible by Archangel Raphael and his healing angels. We thank all the guides friends and helpers, all the angelic realm and all the ascended masters and the divine for their presence amongst us, for all the cleansing and clearings, protection, guidance, healings, messages that were passed on and everything else that is for our highest good. I ask for the golden circle of protection to be placed around each of you and until we meet again may the angels bless you. Thankyou.

HOW TO WORK WITH YOUR SPIRIT GUIDES (MENTAL MEDIUMSHIP)

Mental Mediumship is the correct term to use when we are asking for our guides to give us messages to do a reading for another person. Our guides work with us in a variety of ways to give us information with which to share with those that we are working with. The messages that they bring us can seem like our own imagination as mental Mediumship is perceived within our own minds and it is then. For the novice, beginner, it is difficult at first to decipher as to whether it from spirit or in their own imagination.

I personally find that when we ask for our highest and best guide to give us a message, the first thing that comes to mind will be the correct one. This is before we can start to try and work the message out, which can completely altar the true meaning if we allow our mind to interfere with the process.

As always prior to any spiritual/psychic work make sure that you have already done all of your cleansings, clearings and protection work for yourself as well as for the room that you are working in before you open the class or do anything else.

I always do a meditation prior to any work with spirit especially with students as it is important to be able to get into the "zone" to perceive messages from the higher realms. Our brain waves need to be in an altered state and so we need to be deeply relaxed to be able to gain the information that our guides are bringing to us. At least 20 minutes is the recommended time for this to occur in, although for anyone that has been doing this for a period of years may find that they are able to instantaneously achieve this. But, please do not do that to your students, to make them try to instantly get messages without meditating, as they will find it too difficult and give up and leave class with the belief that they are not any good at Mediumship or utilising their psychic abilities. That would be a great shame as they may never ever try another class with anyone again, and you will have stopped their spiritual progress! (Not good karma)

On that note, anyone can become a medium with enough good training, an open mind and a willingness to allow the meditation process to get them to that relaxed state in which they are then able to perceive their spirit guides.

First ask your students at the end of the meditation, before opening their eyes, to ask for their highest and best clairvoyant/clairaudient guide to come to give them a message for each person that is in the room. Some of them may get their messages whilst seated and others will prefer to get them as they go. Either way is fine at first, but as they advance it is preferable to get them as they go. I have found that some students will get their messages whilst seated for up to two years coming to regular weekly classes before feeling confident in themselves to just get them on the spot standing in front of the person that they are reading.

I learnt a lot whilst being a student myself, for over seven and a half years, in the weekly classes that I attended. I will allow students when they first come into a class for a while to get their messages seated, but they must stand in front of the person to deliver the messages. With them getting use to standing in front of the other student, they are then that step closer to getting them standing in front of the person.

The first thing that the student should say to the person that they wish to deliver a message to is to ask "May I come to you". This gives the "reader" permission to get information for the client.

Messages may come in the form of an image within their own mind. For some it will be a word, or a sentence that they hear, or perhaps seen written on a blackboard or similar. Others will get a feeling in their body, and yet others will just have a feeling of knowing what is going on with the person that they are reading. With a feeling or pain in their body it may feel like it is their own, but if they did not have it prior to asking for a message for them, then that is usually a good sign that it is a message. Once the message is delivered I always say thank you for the message and ask for Archangel Raphael to please remove the feeling from me and give healing to who it belongs to.

It takes time to learn to trust that what you are getting is in fact a message from your guide and not from your own imagination. I find that the first thing that you perceive, will always be the correct information and you should not second guess it. When we second guess ourselves, we usually then have our conscious/logical mind stepping in, and we do not want that to happen. The conscious mind has finite information not unlike a computer, whilst when we can tap into knowledge from higher beings in can then become an infinite source and wealth of information and knowledge.

This like all the following exercises takes a lot of practise to get really good at it and at the very least the personal growth from doing all of these different modalities in learning to "read others" will also allow us to explore ourselves in a much deeper way. You will find then a much calmer and peaceful place within yourself and that is worth more than anything else in my opinion!

I actually try to do mental Mediumship every second week in class as it is the basis of learning how to read for others no matter what the tool you may be utilising, such as oracle cards, flowers etc.

CRYSTAL DIAMOND PALACE

Now see golden light coming through the ceiling, touching the floor and it now spreads right across the floor and then a myriad of coloured lights cascade flowing down it forming the rainbow bridge. Then the rainbow bridge spreads wider and wider and large fluffy clouds come down and one lands right in front of you. You can see that it is quiet yielding, but strong and firm at the same time, so it will easily hold you.

So you step into your fluffy cloud and as you sit in it, you feel it yielding to the shape of you. It's so comfortable you just relax into it and then effortlessly it starts to go up the rainbow. You may want to take notice of what colour you are going up on. As it goes up and takes you through the ceiling, through the roof and out into the sky the rainbow expands out further. The rainbow road is very broad and you feel as if your cloud has been magnetised to the rainbow. It keeps taking you up higher and higher and it is like the cloud has a protective auric field around it.

No matter what the temperature is on the outside you can't feel it. You sense that it is cold out there but you are not feeling it as it is just keeping you at a nice temperate temperature, just perfectly warm.

You can see as look down below at the houses and the cars on the roadways that they get smaller and smaller as the cloud continues along the rainbow, taking you up higher and higher and you can see the suburban sprawl and you also see the city landscape. You can see all the mountains and the forests and the rivers that run through them. You look across and see the vast ocean. The cloud goes higher and higher along the rainbow, and you can no longer make out the details of the cars on the roadways or the houses as there is just the greenery of the landscape, and the ocean.

Now you are getting higher and you are going into the wispy little white clouds up through the storm clouds but you are not wet, as you are in your protective shielding, you are in your cloud pod that is travelling along the rainbow bridge.

You continue going up higher and higher, you notice that you are getting faster now in your cloud, and you go right up through the earth's atmosphere. You are into the night sky now, and beyond that out into outer space and you also know that you can breathe perfectly easily here.

You look across at the moon and it looks very close now and you know that even though your cloud is going super-fast like a racing car, you feel like you are sitting still as it is so smooth. It is completely effortless for you and you just sit here and relax in your cloud, going along the rainbow. You look across and you can see all the different planets, Mercury and Mars, Venus, Jupiter, Saturn, Pluto, Uranus, Neptune, Chiron and all the stars are so much brighter here you see the milky way, you look ahead and you can see that the rainbow is going right through the milky way. It is so bright here it is so peaceful.

You can feel the energy here in outer space, it is very tranquil and peaceful. And now your cloud on the rainbow is taking you right through the Milky Way. There are so many bright stars. You can see further ahead there is a huge tube of white light and the rainbow is heading straight into. You go straight into it and as you do, it whirrs and it whooshes as you go through it. It is so bright in here, you know you are being taken to a different time and place.

As you go out the end of the tube of white light and get to the other side you see that you are in a different solar system, a different galaxy, a different universe, you see a bright light ahead of you that the rainbow is heading straight towards, with you and your cloud on it. You know that you have come to a safe and sacred place. The bright light is ahead and you can just start to make out that it is a beautiful crystal diamond palace. It is huge. You look across at the different types of planets so brilliantly coloured, and the nebula, it is very pretty here.

You sense that your cloud is starting to slow down. You can see that the rainbow butts right up against a beautiful pearlescent roadway that leads right up to the crystal diamond palace. Your little cloud goes right up to that pearlescent roadway and halfway onto it, as if it is parked there. You hop out of your cloud and walk along this beautiful pearlescent roadway. You are walking towards the crystal diamond palace and you can see that there are seven stairs that lead up into the entrance, and when you get there, I want you to count the seven stairs as you are going up them. One, two, three, feeling so free of all your daily activities and thoughts, four, five, feeling lighter, six and seven, feeling bright and free and happy as you enter into this beautiful place.

Everything you see in here has been carved out of the crystal diamond, all the rooms have been carved out of it, everything that you see. You will see in the central chamber, chairs that have been carved from this beautiful crystal diamond. Go towards the central chamber where you see a circle of chairs that are carved, and sit in the one you feel most drawn to and as you sit in it even though it is firm it feels as though it was carved just for you to sit in.

Your feet are flat on the floor here, you can feel the energy, the higher vibrational energy of the crystal diamond. It starts to permeate now through your feet and you might feel the gentle vibrational humming coming right up through you. You can hear crystal humming above your head and then a myriad of lights begin to cascade down to you. Some of them bright and vibrant, some of them are so subtle and translucent in colour.

They go through and around you and your auric field. You may notice that some of them correspond to your chakras as they touch those areas, and others maybe the opposite, there are many different things that these rays of light do for healing. This is a healing chamber and so the crystal diamond healing energy is permeating right through you, and so are all of these beautiful colours.

Know that you will only absorb exactly what you need and no more. This beautiful energy continues to permeate through you. Reds and oranges, yellows and greens, blues, purples, pinks, in an assortment of all different shades.

A beautiful golden light now comes down and touches your crown chakra and gently flows all through you, going directly down through the chakra column, all these other lights are interplaying within your auric field. You have been so busy looking at all these lights and feeling the vibration going right through you that you didn't notice higher beings coming in.

Archangel Raphael now stands in front of you and he has a small crystal diamond in his hand. With your permission, he will place it within your third eye. This is to help you with your clairvoyant vision. He has two more and with your permission he will place them behind your physical ears, for your clairaudient hearing. This is done, in the hope that, with raising your vibrational level and opening your clairvoyance and your clairaudience, that if you do not already perceive the higher beings, then one day you will be able to hear him, his brethren, the angelic realm, the ascended masters as well as your highest and best guides and any other higher beings that you wish to, or they wish to, commune with you.

Archangel Chamuel now steps forward and places a beautiful rose pink crystal diamond right within your thymus, into that chakra to help you with unconditional love. This is so that you will easily be able to feel this, firstly for yourself and then towards others.

Archangel Raphael steps forward again with you, standing in front of you, and you may ask, in your mind mentally, for whatever healing it is that you currently need at this time. It can be anything physically, mentally, emotionally, spiritually. I will leave you for a minute to be with Archangel Raphael to ask whatever it is that is required by you. You can also handover to Archangel Raphael any burdens that you have been carrying and say "Thank you for the lessons that they have brought, but I give it back as I no longer require it." Now see that energy being transmuted into a beautiful clear crystal diamond, it is handed back to you as such. Now you are able to see the value of the lesson that it has bought you. We thank Archangel Raphael and Archangel Chamuel and all the other higher beings that were here today assisting with our healing process.

As we stand up and walk back towards the front door of the palace, there is an entity standing in the doorway, he has a gift for you and places it in your hand. We thank the entity for allowing us entry into this beautiful, sacred place. We also give thanks for the beautiful gift that is being placed into your hands.

We count the seven stairs as we walk back down them. One, two, three, feeling much freer and lighter, four, five, six, feeling happiness growing within your heart. Six and seven, feeling the joy of your inner child as you walk back down that pearlescent roadway, where you see your fluffy cloud waiting for you at the top of the rainbow.

You are taking in the beauty of your surroundings and you feel like you are so happy and free that you could almost skip along that pathway like you did when you were a young child. You are back now to where the fluffy cloud waits, and you step back into your fluffy cloud feeling yourself very firmly seated. Then it effortlessly and quickly takes off along the rainbow. You may be on a different colour coming back to the one coming up.

You take one last, long, look around at this beautiful place that you have come to as your cloud very swiftly takes you along the rainbow. You can now see that white tube of light and, as you enter it, it is whirring as you go all the way through it, knowing that it is going to bring you back to the same time and place you that came from. Then you exit out of it and you are back going through the Milky Way. The lights are so bright here from the stars it is so beautiful. You feel yourself settling back down and relaxing more as you know that you heading towards home.

You are now looking out across at all the different planets in our solar system. You can see the earth looking very small because we are still so far away. I want you to visualize and ask for Archangel Raphael to put his emerald green healing blanket right around the whole planet to heal the entire planet and all the inhabitants. We also ask for the rose pink ray of unconditional love to completely surround it. We are getting closer and closer now. We are getting towards the earth's moon and there is a shooting star that goes across the sky. So quickly, make a wish on it.

Going past the earth's moon and we are very quickly now getting very close to the earth and the cloud slows down ever so slightly as it comes back into the earth's atmosphere. You can now see the clouds, you are going right down through the clouds now. You are now looking out across the earth's landscape, you can see the ocean and the land mass. Now you can start to make out the mountains and the trees, the cityscape, suburban sprawl, the rain is falling but it is not touching you. You are still within the auric field of protection of the cloud. The cloud is flying down further and further going very slowly now, very gently as it comes back down through the roof that you had come out from, coming right down now and very gently placing you back in your seat. You now feel yourself very firmly back in your seat, keeping with you all of the healing and any knowledge that you attained and also the gift that was given to you. Just very gently allow yourself to feel all the way back in your physical body, stretch and slowly open your eyes when ready.

LESSON 2

HOW TO GIVE AN ORACLE CARD READING:

I prefer to use five different decks of oracle cards to teach for students to learn with. Firstly, you will need to have a table large enough to lay out all of the decks in their entirety. I like a variety of topics on the decks, but, I make sure that they are always positive with the messages and imagery for this workshop. I usually utilise at least two different angel decks, a faerie deck, a unicorn deck and a mermaid deck. The reason that I use five different decks and not just the one, and to not get the students to take five cards from the one deck is that the students may already have it at home. This makes sure that the student needs to rely upon their own intuition and not the memory of what the cards mean.

Now lay out your first deck of cards and spread them straight across in a line face down, now underneath that lay out the second deck, then the third, fourth and finally the fifth deck. You can add more decks if you like as there are no rules, but I find that students can manage five cards nicely without feeling too overwhelmed by the process.

I ask for each student to pick their own cards, but then I get another person to read the cards for them. Now get the students to "intuitively feel" which card from each of the decks that they need to choose to give them information on what it is that they need to know about now and in the near future.

Make sure that you always try to get a different person to read for them with the cards each time you do this. This is so that the students can stretch themselves to get more information than they may have previously known about their fellow students.

I always have certain decks in the same placements, and I put the first deck at the bottom that I feel has the most earthly energy, and then the next one, and so on finishing with what I feel is the highest vibration which is always an angel deck. I do like Doreen Virtue's Angel decks as the imagery is very beautiful and you can intuitively pick up positive messages from them very easily. So, why not use two different types as it finishes the reading for a person on a positive note.

Ask the students now one at a time to choose their cards by picking them up in the order that they were laid out. I ask them not to look at their own cards until after all of the readings have been completed. I find that this helps the other person that is reading for them, so that they do not feel under pressure as to whether they have got it right or not as their "client" may have preconceived ideas about what the cards represent in their life at the current moment. The problem with that is that we can get it really wrong for ourselves as it is always subject to our judgement which can stop our intuitive abilities gaining that extra information. If we are in a positive frame of mind, then we will see everything in a good light, and if we are in a negative frame of mind, then obviously we will see things as not so happy and positive.

When we do readings for others we tend to be able to be more open and subjective to what is actually there and not judge the information as to whether it is positive or negative, but that it is the truth that is being brought to light. Do always be careful though, as to how the messages are delivered. In life we will always have difficult times at some point, and whilst that information needs to be delivered, we do not need to be overly blunt about it. But, I always say, "forewarned is forearmed". This means that if we get the heads up as to an unpleasant situation coming up in a person's life, we are then able to do something about it.

Now get each student to pass their cards onto the person that has been chosen to do their reading for them. I will either get them to give it to the first or the second person on their left or on their right. I change this on a weekly basis to try and make sure that they do not read for the same person each week. I also try to make sure that I do not get the same person to go first, so as to allow the others to be a bit out of their comfort zone too.

If you are teaching group sessions, then when your students first start you will find that they may need your help for interpreting what they are getting in a message. Depending how their intuition mainly works is how they will get their information for the message. The cards tend to generally help more with visuals with clairvoyance, and something in the imagery on the card may stand out more than anything else. That piece of imagery will form the message along with whatever else the person thinks or feels about it. You will find that not everything on the card will be relevant and some cards may give you hardly anything, whilst others are a goldmine of information where you will just continually keep getting more.

The more frequently that you do oracle card readings, like all other modalities, you will find that everyone gets better at it. I also find oracle card readings are the best thing to start with when I have a new student in class as it gives them a focal point to gain information as it is easier than doing something like mental Mediumship.

If your group seems to be getting stuck on trying to bring through information utilising the cards, I find the following exercise an easy and interesting way to get them all to relax more with it and go with the flow a lot more.

First choose any oracle card deck and put one card down. Now get them to just quickly throw out anything that comes to them of what they think that particular card says to them. Do not have this as a reading for anyone, but just play with the cards in a general manner. Continue doing this so that they get quicker and no longer feel self-conscious. Remember, that there is very little symbolism that is hard and fast as to what it means, so you can allow the students almost free reign as to the interpretation that they are getting on any card. You may want to change the deck part way through so that if that deck didn't resonate with them, then hopefully the next one will.

When it comes to symbolism there are few things that are hard and fast with meanings as I like to help students unravel their own symbolic dictionary. So, I will say to the student when they are asking "what does that mean", I ask what does a "whatever" mean to them? The last thing that I want to have happen is for a person to get stuck and caught up with "book knowledge". When this occurs, it means that a person is purely relying on memory and not on intuition.

Water is one thing that will always mean that it relates to the emotions in some way. Take notice of the state of the water as to how to interpret it. For example, if the water that is seen is the ocean and the sea is rough and the waves are high and crashing, then stormy seas are quite literally ahead for the person receiving that message. If it is calm and the waves are gently rolling in, then it means that emotionally that the person is coming into a more peaceful existence in their life. If the water is murky, then it is time for them to look within or perhaps get some extra help in order to go through a period of cleansing themselves from past situations. Please always tread carefully when delivering messages of this nature as people can take offense. After all, we all have life's ups and downs and it's only natural to experience things that may be difficult to overcome for a period of time. Nothing can be overcome overnight, but it takes a process that sometimes cannot be rushed.

MEDITATION 2

TAKING YOUR POWER BACK/ CUTTING CORDS/FORGIVENESS

Now see yourself standing in the middle of a beautiful green field with rolling hills all around you. There is a forest ahead. You can see an opening in the forest where a path meanders through it. The sun is high in the sky and you can feel it gently warming you. The grass is thick and lush under your feet as you start to walk towards the pathway that leads into the forest.

As you enter the forest it is slightly cooler in temperature, but the sun shines through the canopy of the tree tops that have formed an archway over the top of your head and you can feel the warmth on your shoulders.

You take notice of all of the wildflowers that line the pathway and you can see a variety of beautiful colours, shapes, sizes and types. Also varying styles of toadstools and mushrooms along the path and further into the forest at the bottom of the trees. You see many beautiful ferns in so many different varieties including maiden hair, fish fern, bracken and tree ferns, that are taller and broader in size the deeper that you travel into the forest. It is the same with all of the plants and trees and as you look up, the trees are so tall here that they seem to go on forever. You know that you have entered a very ancient part of the forest now as you can feel the energies from eons ago like an echo through the breeze that goes through the trees.

You start to hear the faint sound of running water. As you continue walking the sound of water gets louder. A few more steps ahead and then you see that the forest opens up to reveal a river. As you get closer to the river you can see that the water looks pristine and absolutely crystal clear. You listen as the water gurgles over the rocks, these have been smoothed of any jagged edges through the passage of time of eons past. You can see that further along the river is a beautiful waterfall that is feeding this river. The sound of the waterfall gets louder and louder with every step that you take along the pathway that goes beside the riverbank. You look at the majesty of the waterfall as it flows over the rock face, and if you look closely at it, you will be able to see the spirit of the lady of the waterfall in the cascading water.

You can see that this pathway that goes along the riverbank, goes in and behind the waterfall. You follow this to explore what lies behind it. As you walk in behind the waterfall you are surprised to see a large cavern that has seven steps that lead down into it and it is quite well lit up down here.

Before you go down the steps, stand behind the waterfall and feel the refreshing energy radiating out from it. You can feel it cleansing and rejuvenating your auric field and you very slowly now turn around for it to completely cleanse all around you.

You can see that cavern is well lit and you slowly walk down the seven steps counting them as you go down each one. One, two, three, you are now feeling more relaxed with each step that you take. Four, five, six, feeling very calm, relaxed and comfortable, seven, you are now walking across the floor of the cavern.

You now see somewhere here in the cavern a giant computer screen that is bigger than any computer screen than you have ever seen before. Walk over to it and place your hands upon the screen. Now, in your mind, say to yourself, "I now release all negative and/or unwanted thoughts, thought patterns and all self-sabotage patterns from my subconscious mind and anything else that is holding me back from me being able to reach and fulfil my highest potential in this lifetime."

You may see words, sentences, phrases or even pictures downloading from you and onto the screen. Don't worry about what they say or bother with reading them as you are in the process of letting them go. Feel yourself now empty and free of negativity.

Now, either type using the keyboard or use the pen that is there to write on the screen as many positive thoughts, words, phrases and mantras that you can think of. You can also ask for help with this process from your highest and best guides and any other higher being that can, and is willing, to assist you with this task. (Allow yourself about half a minute or so with this task before continuing on your journey)

Now step away from the computer screen and start to walk towards the back wall of the cavern. As you get closer you see a golden door appear, and then as it senses your energy it magically opens. As the door swings open it reveals a golden lit chamber of golden floors, walls and ceilings and the room glows with a golden light.

You enter and feel completely safe, knowing that you are in a safe and sacred place. The door closes behind you as you take a few steps into the room. In your mind, now, call forth your highest and best spirit guides, friends, and helpers, along with Archangel Michael to help with everything that we are about to do.

Now in your mind see the person that you most need to unhook from, take back your power, cut cords from and lastly, to forgive. If there are a few different people that you need to this work with, then choose the one that is uppermost in your mind. Once you have chosen your person, then ask them to come in through the golden door on the opposite side of the room. As they enter, they must stand there, and do as you say and just stand there, as this is your sacred place and they can do nothing without your permission.

The first thing that you need to do is to check yourself for any hooks that this person may have placed within you. Ask all of the higher beings that are with you to please help with this process. Some of the hooks may be tiny, whilst others may be very large. You may have some on the front of you, some behind you, some may even be on top of your head, and in fact they can be anywhere. As you pull them out, do it slowly so that they will heal immediately and leave no scar. You will see that there is a large vat of acid next to you for you to place the hooks into, as hooks are always negative and should be destroyed and never placed into anyone for any reason. Take about a minute to do this, to continually scan for more hooks so that you are completely free of them.

Now ask for all of the higher beings helping to continue with unhooking you as we go onto the next step of this process.

Now, in your mind reach out your hands towards them, without touching them, and with the thought of taking back your power. Ask first for your power to be cleansed by St Germains Violet Flame of Transmutation so that only your pure essence will be returning back to you and nothing else. Sense your power now coming back to you through St Germains Violet Flame of Transmutation and entering you. You now feel the strength of your power returning into you and feel it now growing within.

Now see the cord that runs between you and the other person that is attached around your midriff area. You can see a pair of golden scissors near you, just pick them up to cut the cord. Make sure that you leave a few inches on you of the cord and the same at the other end for the other person when you cut the cord. If you are having difficulty with this exercise, then ask for Archangel Michael to help to cut it for you with his blue flaming sword.

Now put the length of cord that is left, the piece that was cut away from you both, into the vat of acid beside you so that it is destroyed and cannot reconnect with you at that level. If you so choose, you can tell the other person that they are welcome to reconnect at a higher level with you than the connection that was previously there. Otherwise, just leave it as it is. Now ask for the golden divine white light to heal, seal and block it from reconnecting.

This last step that you are about to do, you may have to fake it before you can make it! So, don't worry if you feel yourself resisting, but just allow the process to happen. In your mind repeat after me and say to them, "I forgive you for all past hurts, words, and deeds that affected me, as I now understand that it was a learning experience for us both. I now release you and let you go in love and light for your highest good. We are both free. Now see them walk back out of the golden door at the opposite side of the room where they came in.

You are now once again alone in the golden room with your highest and best guides and Archangel Michael. Golden energy begins swirling from the floor and continues to swirl all around you and goes right up through your auric field, going right around you, faster and faster. As it continues going faster it is getting rid of all of the debris and dross from you, letting go of all of the negativity from the past. It is completely cleaning you and raising your vibrational rate of being with having your aura infused with the golden energy.

You now feel free from the past and uplifted, cleansed, strengthened and purified. Now turn around to exit the room. As you walk towards the door, it opens as if magically sensing your energy.

We thank Archangel Michael, as well as your highest and best guides for helping with this exercise today.

We re-enter the cavern and walk all the way through it towards the seven steps that go up to the back of the waterfall. We count them as we go up them. One, two, three, feeling lighter, freer, happier and joyful with each step that we take upwards. Four, five, six and seven. Now you are back at the top of the stairs of the cavern facing the waterfall again feeling the refreshing energy coming off from it as it purifies and invigorates your auric field. You slowly turn around so that the energy goes right throughout your entire aura and energy system.

Now go around to the other side of the waterfall from where you came in and where you will find an alcove with a reflective mirror. As you stare at yourself in the mirror, allow your gaze to shift and as you do you will see a happy future event. Allow yourself a minute or so to do this.

Now walk back along the pathway that you came in on, behind the waterfall and back outside the along the riverbank. Feel the warmth of the sun on you, and watch as the sunshine dances upon the river as the water rushes by, as you continue to walk along the path by the side of the river.

You can see the pathway that leads through the forest, the one you came in on and you head towards it. Somehow the forest seems brighter and more alive with bird life than when you came through it earlier. You feel lighter, with more joy in your heart, and you can feel it filling to overflowing with happiness with every step that you take on your walk through the forest.

Further ahead you see a myriad of beautiful butterflies in different colours and hues that appear to be leading you back out of the forest. They appear to be doing some sort of choreographed dance in the air as they continue to fly further ahead down the pathway. It all looks so beautiful.

Before you realise it, you see the forest open up to reveal the green grassy meadow that you started the journey from. You walk over to the spot where you first arrived in this place and find yourself magically transported all the way back to the room that you are physically sitting in. You retain all of the good feelings that you gained during the meditation and allow yourself to gently come all the way back and then slowly open your eyes when ready.

You can do this meditational exercise as many times as you feel that you need to. If, like most of us, there are a lot of people that you feel the need to this with, I highly recommend writing a list and then one by one work through it. Sometimes you may need to this meditational exercise more than once with the person to completely change the way that you feel. As previously said, the payoff for you to continually keep working on yourself is huge. After all, what have you got to lose except for some old emotional baggage that is doing you no favours by staying within you!

LESSON 3

TEA LEAF READINGS

This is one reading modality that most students really enjoy. I'm not sure if it's because they get to have a hot cup of tea and some goodies to eat! For this reason I try to know when it is a student's birthday as it is something nice to do for them, to have tea party in their week of their special day. I ask each of the students if they would like to bring in a small plate of food to share for the day.

Firstly make sure that you have a large enough table to hold all of the tea cups with saucers, the tea pot and all of the plates of food, and remember sugar, spoons and milk. I make sure that everything is set up ready to go except for the hot water in the tea pot, and if it is hot weather, then keep the milk in the fridge until the tea has been poured. I do make sure that I have the tea pot ready with the correct amount of tea leaves for the amount of students that are there for the class lesson.

The tea that I prefer to use is Madura. I find the size of the tea leaf small enough to make it easier to "see things" in it. It is also a tea that has only two percent caffeine, making it usually acceptable to those who do not like to have any caffeine in their diet.

After the meditation, go and put hot water into the tea pot and get the milk and place it on the table. Allow the tea too steep for a minute or so and ask if anyone prefers a weak tea as if they do pour a cup for them fairly quickly. I always say the person's name in my mind when I am pouring them their tea. I pour all of the tea into the cups and then look to see if each one has enough leaves. If not, I mentally again say that person's name in my mind and then get a spoon and get some leaves out of the pot and put them into their cup. They can now all enjoy their tea and the refreshments. This is a good time for everyone with taking turns to talk about their experience with the meditation whilst they are waiting for each other to finish.

Now that everyone has finished their cup of tea it is time to get the tissues, now leave the cup on the table and put a tissue evenly onto the saucer. *Make sure that they have drunk all of the tea and that every cup is fairly empty of liquid, otherwise tea will go everywhere! Now get the saucer with the tissue and place it upside down onto the top of the cup. Now flip it over so that the cup is upside down on the saucer. You now need to turn the cup without lifting it off the saucer three full turns clockwise. It easy to use where the handle is as a guide as to where you count each turn until the three is complete. Do not steady the saucer with your other hand as the way the tissue is shaped will form part of the reading. Do not pick it up when you have finished this process as you are going to pass it onto another student for them to read your cup and saucer and you will read their cup and saucer.

Get all of the students to hand the cup and saucer over to the next person, and choose whether everyone goes to the left or to the right. Once you have someone else's in front of you, gently take the cup off the saucer so as not to disturb how the tissue has scrunched and put it down upright next to the saucer.

What the saucer depicts to you is what is hidden from the querent. This may be good or unpleasant, but as I always say forewarned is forearmed. We look for how the tissue is scrunched and how it forms shapes, also how the tea stains onto it forming images as well tea leaf formations on it. We can sometimes find a wealth of hidden information here. Remember that this is what is hidden from the person, so they are likely to say that what you are giving them is incorrect as they do not have knowledge about it as yet.

I get each of the students to read only the saucer first as they all take turns.

Now, to look at the tea cup. Generally what you can see in this will show you what is likely to occur for the person now and for the next twelve months. You need to look at timing in the cup by dividing it into four sections, almost like cutting an apple into quarters. Starting at the handle, but you need to know whether the person drank holding it by the handle in their right or their left hand. This determines where you start the reading. Most people are right handed, so I will explain it for right handed people, but you only need to reverse this for the left handed person's reading.

As you are holding the cup with your right hand, imagine it in quarters that go from the rim and all the way down into the bottom. At the handle is now and at what would be on a clock the six o'clock mark being three months away. From that, now go to what would be nine o'clock and at that point is 6 months away. At what would be twelve o'clock, that is nine months away, then back to the handle is twelve months away. Anything that is right in the centre at the bottom of the cup, basically has an influence over the entire twelve months to come.

Looking at the tea leaves to do a reading is trying to make out shapes that may not be overly sharp in detail, but remind you of a particular object, thought or feeling. It is kind of like watching clouds go by and making things out of them. Just allow your imagination to flow with this. Sometimes the tea leaves bunch up in a heap, but you can see shapes on top of the heap if you allow yourself to just play with this method. Tea leaf reading may take a few times for some to get the hang of it before they feel they can get much out of it for a reading. Once again, practise makes perfect!

MEDITATION 3
UNICORN VALLEY

To begin this meditation either lay flat or sit upright in a chair with your feet flat on the floor and hands gently resting in your lap. Now allow your eyes to gently relax and close. Take a deep breath through your nostrils and exhale through your mouth, and, as you do feel all of your cares and worries go with each outbreath that you take.

Now visualise yourself standing in the middle of a beautiful green field with rolling hills all around you. As you look up into the sky you see hot air balloons in such a great diverse variety of colours. Some of the hot air balloons are predominantly one colour whilst others are multi coloured.

They start to descend, and you can tell that they will soon be landing all around you where you are standing. You already have your eye upon one of the hot air balloons that you feel most drawn to and you start to walk towards where you estimate where it will land in the meadow.

All of the hot air balloons now land gently on the grass. You can see a lot of hot air balloons are heavily weighed down with many sandbags hanging from them. You now climb into the basket of your chosen ride. You now notice that there are words written on the sandbags. You see one that has fear written on it, so you throw it off. As it leaves your basket the hot air balloon starts to rise. You notice that after you threw it away, that the emotion that is written on the sandbag also leaves you, and you also feel lighter. You take another sandbag that says anger and as you throw it away, you find that any anger that has been residing within you also disappears from you. You throw off another sandbag and this one reads disappointment and that feeling now leaves you. You continue throwing off the remaining sandbags, knowing that as you do that, the emotion that you have been holding onto, now also leaves you. Sandbags with the words on them, sadness, grief, revenge, loneliness, unforgiveness, frustration, envy, and with each sandbag being thrown off as the hot air balloon rises you also feel much lighter, freer and unburdened.

As it gets higher and higher you can see for many miles around you. You start to travel above a beautiful forest that surrounds the green, grassy, rolling hills, where you took off in the hot air balloon from. You see a beach beyond the tree line, to the left side of you and the ocean stretches out far beyond where the eye can see. The ocean is so pristine and crystal clear that you can see a very colourful coral reef not too far from the shoreline. Beyond that you can see a huge pod of dolphins. Farther out into deeper water you see some mother whales, with their babies close by their side and to the surface of the water.

The hot air balloon is following along the mountain range as you watch the terrain change from green thick luscious forest to a slightly rocky mountain range. You look further ahead and see snow-capped mountains and tree tops with the landscape covered in a blanket of white. Even though the climate would be cold below, you are sheltered within the basket of the balloon which is keeping you at just a comfortable temperature.

Your balloon continues travelling further along the mountain range and you can see the snow melting and now the mountains are thick and lush and green with trees and thick undergrowth. The hot air balloon begins to very slowly descend. It almost feels as if the balloon is magnetised to where it seems destined to land. You eagerly look further ahead to try and see where you will be landing. In the distance you can see where the thick forest opens up to reveal a massive valley. Running through this valley you can see a very colourful looking river that a beautifully coloured waterfall feeds into it its energy. You see so many horses grazing on the lush green grass as you continue to slowly descend. On a closer look, you are now able to see that they are in fact not horses, but unicorns! Some have foals with them that nuzzle closer to their mothers as they watch the hot air balloons getting ready to land.

It is such a soft landing that you don't even feel a bump as the basket touches down on the ground. You get out of the basket to explore the unicorn valley. One of the unicorns comes up to greet you. As you look into its eyes you feel a warm compassion from them to you of unconditional love. You have the same feeling welling in your heart for them which makes you feel warm inside.

The unicorn walks with you and ushers you towards the rainbow coloured river. As you get closer you see that it is not water that runs through this river, but liquid energy! You notice that the rainbow of colours that cascade down the waterfall and flow gently into the river is the same order as the colours of your corresponding chakras in your energy system.

You walk right up to the edge of the river bank and walk into the river. You know somehow that when you lay down in the river, immersed with the liquid colours, that you will be able to breathe perfectly normally and easily, and that you are safe and well protected in this place. As you lay down into the healing energy of the rainbow river, you place the top of your head into the violet light colour of the stream, indigo blue flows through your third eye chakra. This is located between the eye brows. Light blue flows through your throat chakra and you notice how each of the colours seems to dissolve away and flush out any energy blockages or negative energies in those areas and it gets transmuted into positive energy almost immediately going down stream.

A beautiful rose pink flows through and around the thymus, and a beautiful deep emerald green through the heart chakra and surrounding area. A pretty peach/apricot colour flows through your soul star chakra which is located between the heart and the solar plexus which links you with the inner sun within the earth. Sunshine yellow travels through the solar plexus whilst a vivid orange like the sun now goes through the sacral chakra. A brilliant red flows through the base chakra also cleansing and removing all blockages and revitalising and re-energising your physical body and your entire energy system.

Whilst allowing the rainbow river to help clear your energy system it is also the perfect time for you to release and let go of any thoughts and/or emotions that you have been holding onto. This is as simple as just saying to yourself, "I now release and let go of anything and everything that I have been holding onto that is not for my highest good, including negative thoughts, negative thought patterns, negative belief systems, self-sabotage patterns, negative emotions and anything that I have created within myself because of them."

Now feel all of these things emptying out from you and leaving you and flowing down stream. All of the beautiful coloured energies that flow into you now replace all that has been released, raising your vibrational rate to a much higher frequency.

You notice how you are feeling much lighter and freer with a more positive attitude about yourself and your life. (Allow one minute of silence to allow for anything else that you feel that you need to do, or just enjoy these energies before continuing)

Now sit up in the river and feel the crystal clear clarity in your energy fields. You get up now, and walk back onto the riverbank and have a big stretch. One of the unicorns' walks up to you and you reach out towards it with your hands to caress its face. It lowers its head to you and releases its horn into your hands as a gift to you. Don't worry, as the unicorn will quickly grow another one to replace the one you now have in your hands, as it is feeding on the grass that has been fed by the rainbow river giving it magical healing properties. Keep the horn that has been given to you to use for yourself, for your own healing purposes, or, if you choose you can also share this with others to help heal them too.

Thank your unicorn for its generous gift of itself as you continue now to walk across the soft green grass to where your balloon awaits you for the return trip.

You get back into the basket of the hot air balloon and you notice that there are different sandbags with something different written on them than the ones that you released earlier. You again start to throw them off so that the balloon begins to ascend and you take another look at the beauty of this place. You marvel at how soft and luxurious the green grass is here, and the beautiful colours of the rainbow river, the waterfall, how the colours never get muddied up together, but each stay a clear colour that remains true to their hue and vibration.

The balloon rises higher and higher with each sandbag that is tossed off. You notice that the unicorns are picking up the sandbags and throwing them into the rainbow river and you understand that this is for them to be cleansed and purified into something more positive.

You begin to drift away from where the unicorns are standing watching you leave their valley. You continue to travel back the same way you came. The terrain below changes from the green mountains, to rocky cliff tops, to snowy mountains and tree tops that are in the forest there. Once again you cannot feel the coldness below as the hot air balloon basket keeps you at a lovely comfortable temperature, no matter where you travel within it. Gradually as you travel along the mountain range, you see the snow melting and revealing the lush forest below. As you look further afield, you look out at the vast deep ocean and see, way out, a family of whales, and a bit closer to shore, the massive pod of dolphins that you had seen earlier on your trip, going to the unicorn valley. You enjoy the feeling of being able to see so much of the landscape that is in this magical terrain. You can see farther ahead of you the familiar rolling hills that has the forest edging around it. You can feel the hot air balloon begin to descend a little bit at a time, going very gently and very slowly. Getting closer to the spot where you took off from on your journey, you try and look further ahead to where you haven't seen or been yet on the other side of the forest. But, you are nearly ready to touch down on the ground in the basket of the hot air balloon. The basket lands ever so lightly that you don't even realise that you have landed, as you didn't feel a bump as your basket touched the earth.

Remember to make sure that you keep your gift of the unicorn's horn with you, before you jump out and leave the basket of the hot air balloon. You notice how light and agile you are as you leap out and onto the soft green grass of the meadow. Walking over to where you first stood in the meadow you notice how much better you feel than when you first started this journey.

Now to ground yourself. Visualise, about six inches below your feet, where your earthstar chakra resides, see roots going from your feet into your earthstar chakra, this makes it spin faster to its correct vibrational frequency. It then shoots roots down into the centre of the heart of mother earth where it links into the highest vibrational crystal kingdom to centre it. You now feel grounded, and whenever needed you can draw up earth's vital life force energy of the highest vibrational frequency, for your physical body, for optimum health and wellbeing in re-energising it.

When you are ready, allow yourself to gently stretch and wriggle your fingers and toes and to slowly open your eyes. Just allow yourself to sit here in a relaxed state before getting up.

You may want to write down any interesting experiences that you had during the meditational journey. Perhaps there were some interesting thoughts when you threw off the sandbags, or what you released in the rainbow river. If you keep a journal of your experiences with each meditation, you will see how you are growing with learning more about yourself and changing.

LESSON 4
PROGRAMMING A CRYSTAL PENDULUM

I always prefer to work with a crystal pendulum as you would be working with another being, as each crystal contains an entity within it. This is why the meditation "meeting your crystals entity" before doing this exercise is best. You can work with metal pendulums, but I have found that your own energies are what is affecting it with the yes and no responses. So, the whole idea of working with a pendulum is to get correct answers to our questions, whether we like the answers that we get or not!

So, the first thing that I do before I look at programming the crystal pendulum or any other for that matter is to clear it of any negative energies, or ties and attachments to any other person, to make it yours. This starts it off with a new energy slate, so to speak. Repeat the following to clear the energies and to disconnect other energies from the pendulum.

I ask please for St. Germain with your violet flame of transmutation, to go right through the entire pendulum and transmute all negative energies into positive energies. I also now ask please, for Archangel Michael with his blue flaming sword, to cut away all cords and links to any other person or being, and to remove them and do whatever is best with those energies for the highest good of all concerned. Now I ask for Archangel Zadkiel to bring your silver violet flame, right through and burn away any remnants of anything that may be left. The pendulum is now clear and ready for programming.

Make sure that you have done the cleansing process before continuing. If you allow someone else to touch your pendulum, then you need to go through the process of cleansing again.

To program your pendulum start with holding it by the top of the cord, chain or whatever it is hanging from and allow it swing of its own accord. Some people like to have their other hand placed underneath, but I do not as I think that it may be influenced by my own energies.

I now ask it, either mentally or out loud, to show me "yes". Your pendulum may swing up and down vertically or horizontally, or it may swing clockwise or anti clockwise. Once you have seen which way it moves for yes, thank it. I now ask for it to show me "no", and thank it. Most times the no answer will be showing the opposite of the yes. So, if yes is clockwise, then the no will be anti-clockwise.

What I do now to check the pendulum for correctness of its yes and no questions and answers, is to ask it something that I know will be an absolute yes answer. Mine is to ask it if I am a female. So, if you are female you would ask that to get your firm yes, and of course if you are a male, then you would change it to male. To check for "no" correctness, I ask the opposite which is am I a male. So, of course you should get the same results with your pendulum swings for the yes and no with your questions as to what it showed you at the programming stage. If, for some strange reason you do not get the answer that you should for your confirmation, then please start all over again starting with the cleansing. I would also go through clearing, cleansing and protecting your energies and that of the room that you are working in beforehand, with also adding for all tricksters and trickster energies to also be removed.

So, you are now ready for your class to begin with their questions. The main thing with this is to make sure that all questions asked must be able to be answered with a definite yes or no answer. Remember to say thank you to the pendulum after it has answered you. You will sometimes get something different happening with the swing of the pendulum, which can mean a maybe, or perhaps if it is a timing issue that the question needs to be worded differently.

Now for the fun to begin! I get each of my students to take turns with their questions and that when they ask, out loud, that everyone also asks their pendulums on their behalf too. So, if you have six students, then all six are asking exactly the same question in the same way. It is interesting to see how many get the same and others the opposite! Just remember that each of these people are students and they are learning to focus their energies which is why the variety of answers. It is always best to try to remain emotionally not involved with the outcome of the answer as you will accidentally taint the outcome. This is not always as easy and as clear cut as one may think. Take for example a student with a potentially serious health condition and they are asking about it. Most of us will be almost willing the pendulum for a happy outcome and with doing that can alter the truth, this can be especially true when asking for ourselves. Continue going round the group with each person taking their turns in order until your time is up for the class.

You can also utilise your pendulum to scan a person's body for any illness or injury and for any chakra imbalances. First get one person to lay onto a healing table and check that they are laying straight on it first. Make sure that you straighten them if they are laying crookedly by gently manoeuvring their legs, head, or whatever part of the body is not straight. Do not do a chakra balancing at this stage.

Now get each student to allow their pendulum to swing in whatever manner to show any imbalance in the energy fields. Each pendulum is held about six inches above the body to scan it. You will find that if the person being scanned has not recently had a chakra balance that every ones pendulums are swinging all over the place making them look like their body is in a terrible state!

Now do a chakra balance for the person. I always perform a chakra balancing prior to every healing as it balances out the entire body, and not just the chakras, so that once you start healing, it goes to where it is really needed and not wasted with trying to balance the energies first.

A chakra balance is a mini healing all by itself. This is great if you only have time to do this and not go into a full healing.

To check how well a chakra balance works you can use a pendulum. First scan a person's body to see where the pendulum swings the most.

Then do a chakra balance. You should see quite a marked difference of before and after the balance. Try this out for yourself.

First start by having your client laying face up on the massage table. Now make sure that they are straight before commencing the balance.

Go to the right side of your client to begin. I like to rub my hands together at this point to get my palm chakras activated to the sensitivity of energies so that I can feel each chakras energy much easier.

All of the chakras must be balanced to match the heart chakra, which is why this is balanced first.

Place your hands about two inches above their heart chakra with your right hand about the same distance above your left hand, directly above the heart chakra. Now feel the energy between each of these hand placements by just gently moving your hands so as to sense the flow of the energy. It may feel like air pressure or two magnets coming together. Then when you feel that you have balanced the heart chakra, then take the right hand and place in the auric field of the base chakra. Now you may feel that you need to slightly bounce the energies with your hands, with either bringing the energy up, or pushing it down if it is too high as long as it matches the energy of the heart chakra.

Once you feel that is right, then place your right hand above the sacral chakra to balance that to the heart chakra. When you feel that is correct, then place your right hand over the solar plexus chakra to match that one too.

Now place your right hand over your left hand to replace it over the heart chakra. The right hand is now holding the energy of the heart chakra in balance whilst the higher chakras are being balanced. Then place the left hand over the crown chakra and balance it to the heart chakra. Now place the left hand over the third eye chakra to balance to the heart. Once that is done, move your left hand over your right hand to finish, and then smooth your hands right across the auric field at about two inches above the physical body.

MEDITATION 4
MEETING YOUR CRYSTALS ENTITY

Now see yourself standing in the middle of a beautiful green field, rolling hills all around you and there is a forest ahead. You see that there is an opening in the forest and you start to walk along the soft green grass towards it. The sun is high in the sky and it is just gently warming you, there are just a few little wispy white clouds in the blue sky. As you walk into the forest you know that this is a sacred forest and you are completely safe on your journey through here.

The pathway is quite wide and there is lots of dappled sunlight that comes through from the canopy at the top of the trees. These trees form an archway over the top of your head. The further you go along the pathway the larger the trees are, the trunks are so broad and the trees are so tall they seem to go on forever.

You look at all the foliage that lines the pathway, the different coloured mushrooms and toadstools in different shapes and sizes and the variety of wildflowers in so many different colours, in reds and oranges and yellow to purples and blues and pinks, white and all shades in between. There are some flowers that look very exotic and you don't remember seeing them ever before, anywhere on the earth.

You start to hear the sound of water ahead, the forest opens up and you can see that there is a river. You can see it is pristine, crystal clear. You look further up to the right, and you can see that there is a bridge that crosses over the river, so you start to walk along the embankment towards the bridge taking in the beautiful sunshine. You are walking on nice soft grass, it has tiny little flowers growing in between it. When you get to the bridge you can see across the other side there is an embankment.

So you walk across the bridge. You see how pretty the river looks with the sunlight dancing upon it. You start walking up the embankment and the grass starts to become sparse, and the soil starts to become sandy and you can smell a sea breeze. When you get to the top you can see a beautiful beach with the sand stretching out in front of you, then a beautiful ocean that is just gently lapping in at the shoreline. The sea is so blue as you are walking along the soft silken sand towards the ocean, but only as far as where the ocean water has left it firm.

You watch the ocean waves just gently rolling in one after the other and you stand here and you feel a beautiful breeze caressing your face, just gently lifting your hair away. As it does this you can feel all your cares and worries just drifting and floating away on the breeze. You feel all the tension in your face and your head leaving you with all of that just floating away on the breeze, you are just letting go now, all your cares and worries just floating away.

With every wave making the sound of lapping water on the shoreline, you can sense yourself feeling more and more relaxed, so calm, so peaceful here, you can feel the sun, and enjoy the warmth of it.

You haven't realised until now that there is crystal on the beach, and when you look at it to the right on the sand, further ahead there it is, your crystal, and it is as huge as a house. So you start to walk towards it, you can see somewhere, that on your crystal there is a doorway. You can easily see it or when you touch on a certain place, a doorway will appear and allow you entry. There might be staircases that lead up all through it. Somewhere in here is the crystals entity. I want you in your mind, if you haven't seen it already, because some of them are quick to appear as they are very excited to meet you. If you haven't met it yet already, send out your intention that you would very much like to meet with it and talk with it, and ask it what role does it play in your life? What can you do together? It could be for a variety of reasons but usually they are with you for one reason. It could be healing, it could be helping you with your psychic abilities or perhaps something else. So I will leave you for a minute or so, so that you can talk with this crystal entity and see what you can learn from it. Then I will return to take you on our return trip back out of the crystal.

It is now time to thank the crystals entity for allowing us into its home, and for speaking with us and sharing their time with us. Turn around now and walk back out the way you came in. Once you are out of the crystal you will see that the door closes. You walk back along the beach, along the sand keeping with you what you shared with the entity.

You walk back along the beach and you stand back in front of the water again, watching the waves just gently rolling in, feeling that calm and that peace as each wave just rolls in. That little wispy wind just caresses your face and hair. You feel a new re-energising energy fill you with each gust of wind that gently caresses your face and hair. Now you turn around and retrace your steps walking back along the sand. You are now going back up the embankment, and looking down it to where you cross over the bridge.

Once you are over the other side of the bridge you start to walk alongside the river. Watching the water dancing over the beautiful soft, smooth pebbles, they have been smoothed over from what were once jaggered rocks over eons of time. You see the main pathway that goes through the forest, the one that you came up on. You start walking down there. Looking once more at all the flowers that line the pathway here, their beautiful colours.

You can see a myriad of butterflies ahead of you, in so many different colours and sizes, they seem to be helping to lead you back out of the forest. You seem to be going out quicker than when you came in. You can now see the opening of the forest that leads back out into the green grassy meadow and full sunshine. You find yourself now in the full sunshine of the green grassy meadow, keeping with you all the feelings of peace. You have been revitalised and have a feeling of calmness and with another step you find yourself very firmly seated in the room. You find yourself all the way back.

LESSON 5

PHOTO READING OF A LIVE PERSON

I prefer to get the students to bring a copy of their photos, or to wrap them in gladwrap to protect them from fingerprints as the oils on our hands can destroy photographs over time and that would be a shame as some photos are irreplaceable with the memories that they hold within them.

With reading a photo of a live person it is similar to doing an absent/distant healing in the way that we tune into the energies. Get your students to give their photo that they have brought to the person next to them. It is best that the photo of the person be someone that they know really well so that they are able to give feedback as to the accuracy of the messages and information perceived.

Once the students have someone else's photo, ask them to ask for their highest and best clairvoyant/clairaudient guide to come and help them with getting a message from the person in the photo. Once again it is somewhat similar to mental Mediumship, but limited to information about the person in the photo.

One important thing to note is, that we are actually not allowed to get information about a person without their permission. So, we are accessing their higher self for permission. They may be happy to share a wealth of information or not much at all. We usually will get information that may let the reader know about their general personality and wellbeing, especially if there may be any health issues. You can access past memories from the person that you are reading from their photograph that can hopefully be recognised by the person that had brought it into class.

The first time doing a reading from a photograph, it may not come that easy, but after several times of doing this style of reading you will find it much easier. Like with most things, the more times you do it, then the better you will become at it.

MEDITATION 5

UNDERWATER PALACE

Now see yourself standing on a beautiful sandy beach. The ocean is very calm and the waves are just gently rolling in at the shoreline. You are standing on beautiful soft silken sand that has been warmed by the sun. The sun is high in the sky and it is a beautiful day, a beautiful blue sky with wispy little white clouds.

When you look down at the ocean you can see that it is perfectly crystal clear. You can see through the water and see the sandy bottom, you can see all the ripples that the waves have made on the sand beneath the ocean. You just breathe in the fresh sea breeze. You feel quiet calm with the ebb and flow of the sea.

You can see that there are seagulls gliding on the air currents above the ocean. As you look out into the distance you can see a pod of dolphins in the ocean. There are so many of them and there seem to be more coming in from different directions.

The beach that you are standing on seems to go on forever to the right and to the left. You can see that there is tropical foliage but your attention remains on the pod of dolphins that is coming in toward the beach. As they are coming closer some of them seem to be excited and they are jumping up out of the water and jumping back in.

You start to walk into the water and you feel that it is just a nice temperature. It is not hot, it is not cold, and it is just perfect. You know that the dolphins are coming to meet you. You start walking in, and you get to about waist deep and the dolphins start to swim in closer. They are so close now, there are a couple that come to urge you to come with them. You go in a bit deeper until you are about chest deep. Now they flank either side of you so you grab hold of the top fin on each of them, right at the base, and you know that you can breathe completely easily in this water, and the dolphins take you in.

As you go into the water with them, other dolphins are in front of you and then as you get a bit deeper in the water they come in behind you, they are underneath you, above you, and all around you. They form like a guard of honour around you, you have become one of their pod. They will completely protect you.

They take you deeper and further into the ocean. You see schools of fish and they quickly dart away. You go over a beautiful coral reef and you see all the colours and shapes and all the little fish that live in the reef and around it. It is so pretty. You continue your journey with the dolphins and they take you deeper and deeper. It is still quiet light in the ocean the sun just permeates all the way through it, the water is just so clear. You can see well ahead of you and all around you even though you are surrounded by dolphins.

A little bit further along they start to veer towards the right and there you see a very bright light. You wonder what it is and as you get closer you can see it is a beautiful crystal palace, here underneath the water. The dolphins start to slow down and as you get closer to the palace. The ones that are in front start to slowly move away as you get closer. You can see that there are stairs that go up into it and the dolphins stop here.

You start to walk up the stairs. We will count them as we go. One, two, three, feeling so calm and peaceful and relaxed, four, and you can see now that there is no water in this palace, five, six, and you are completely dry. Seven, and you enter into this beautiful palace that has been carved out of one giant clear quartz crystal. Everything in here is made of clear quartz. When you walk into here you can see that there are so many beautiful columns here. All the walls are made of clear quartz crystal and they refract every colour there is, so you may in some parts think that some walls may look pink, some purple, some blue, some green.

There is a central chamber here with chairs all around it. You go and sit on one of the chairs and it feels firm yet comfortable, as if it has been carved especially for you to sit in. As you sit here, you feel the vibrational humming of the crystal permeating through your feet and every part of you that is touching the chair. Then you can hear the hum of it from the ceiling as a myriad of lights cascade down from it. Some of them are so refined in colour and hue, some of them are vibrant and rich in colour, some of them spiral right through your chakras others go through different parts. Know that you will only absorb into you the colours that you need and no more they will just pass over you or through you.

Now is the perfect time for you to think to yourself, "I now choose to release all that I have been holding onto that is not for my highest good, and does not serve my highest purpose, and I absorb now all the colours and the energies that are for my highest good". Allow yourself to release all the negativity whether it is thoughts, feelings, emotions, and any pain in the body.

Now a beautiful golden light comes down and touches you on the crown chakra, it gently swirls and as it does it helps to move out and away all blockages, and it clears as it goes through, any debris moves out the nearest chakra exit point. You feel it going right through your head, it is a clearing and calming energy. Now it is clearing and cleansing your third eye chakra and your clairaudience, it almost forms a triangle in your head from the third eye to just behind your two ears. It swirls through clearing your entire head, all congested energy is gone. Any blockages are clearing and this healing energy swirls through, going down the neck now clearing the throat chakra so that you can speak your truth.

This golden energy continues to go down through the tops of the shoulders, right down through the arms, clearing any blocked energy any tensions you can feel in the arms just drops away. As well as going through the chakra column is goes through the skeletal system as well, clearing and strengthening where needed. It also goes through not just the bones but all muscles, ligaments and tissues as it continues to travel down through the chest clearing the thymus, and through the heart chakra where you can have an outpouring of emotions and feelings that are no longer relevant. The beautiful golden energy continues to swirl through your body going through the solar plexus, clearing everything. Going right through all the organs, the digestive system and going down through the sacral spleen chakra now and all related areas. Now down in the base golden energy swirling around here any debris you can see can now just get swept out of the base chakra. It then continues going down through the legs all the way down and right through the feet.

Now filled with the beautiful golden energy and so many different colours vibrations. Now there is a beautiful rose pink ray that enters the heart chakra and the thymus chakra filling you with the highest and purest unconditional love.

You feel yourself completely relaxing. You have let go of all that you no longer needed and you have let go of all your emotional baggage which you chose to let go of today. There may be more, but at least you chose to let go of some today.

And now you get up from the crystal chair and start to walk back out again. When you get to the steps you can see that there is a mermaid. The mermaid is sitting with her tail in the water and her upper half is in the air. She gives you the gift. We thank the mermaid for this beautiful gift. She goes back into the water and swims away.

We walk back down the steps and we count them as we go. One, two, three, we feel so relaxed and comfortable yet refreshed, invigorated and healed. Four, five, six, and our dolphins are all here waiting for us. They gently nuzzle at us. We once more grab hold of the top fins at the base and they take us away from the crystal palace that is here under the water. They flank all around us again and you feel yourself just gliding with them.

You are so relaxed as they take you back through the ocean the way that they brought you in on this journey. You feel so free, so calm, so at one with the pod. You see further ahead another school of small fish, and they quickly scurry off as this massive pod of dolphins are coming towards them.

Once more you are going over the beautiful coral reef, looking at all the beautiful colours here. You notice how you seem to be coming back so much faster than the way you came in, the dolphins are swimming faster, because you are just so relaxed, so comfortable so much at peace. You are feeling a deep inner peace right down to the inner depths of yourself.

Before you know it, you see that we are getting into shallower water. They stop now and they stand you up and you are still completely immersed in water. They now completely surround all around you. Now they release there sonar as this is a healing energy, it helps to break away any stagnant energy and it also helps to sweep away the debris that you are releasing that is not for your highest good. They are making sure that it does not stick anywhere in your auric field. Now they turn around and with their tails they are fanning you, they are making sure that all the debris is being now fanned and swept out of your auric field completely clearing you and cleansing you. You can feel your energy levels raising as they are fanning you they are lifting your energy.

Now they turn around, and they all gently nuzzle at you because they know that it is time for you to go. We thank all these beautiful dolphins for the journey that they took us on and for the healing. As you walk back along out of the water, you notice that with every step you take that as you are getting out of the water that you are completely dry!

Now you are completely back standing on the sand on the shoreline. You turn around and you watch the dolphins swim back into deeper waters. Some of them have their tails out as if they are waving to you, some of them are doing big flips out as they are going out into deeper water. You feel so relaxed watching the dolphins going back.

You turn around to walk along the sand, and with another step, you find yourself magically transported back into your room. You can feel yourself seated very firmly back in your chair. You feel yourself all the way back now and keep with all of the healing gifts received on the journey.

LESSON 6
JEWELLERY (PSYCHOMETRY) READING

Many students really enjoy doing this style of reading. But, I have to say personally, as my students well know, it is not my favourite modality to utilise! I always work in class alongside my students in participating in the readings with all of the modalities, but I have to admit that this is one of the areas where I am not at my best. You will find that something's you will excel at and enjoy and others not so much. We are all different.

The reason why jewellery works so well for some people to read is because metal holds the energy signature of us so easily and records emotions. In particular, the ones who are sensitive to this kind of work can read a wealth of information from the present and the past as a general rule.

Anyway, I start off with a box with a tea towel over it, or you can use something similar, and get all of the students one by one to place a piece of jewellery into it without others seeing what they have put in. This should be done at the beginning of the class prior to the meditation and opening.

The week before this class you should tell the students that the piece of jewellery that they bring should have been worn only by themselves and no one else. This is so that there is no mixture of energies so that the reading isn't muddied by picking up two peoples different energy signatures. As you are working with people who are learning it should be made as simple as possible.

Firstly, ask for your highest and best clairvoyant/clairaudient guide to help you to read the person's piece of jewellery that you are about to receive.

Go around the class and allow them one by one to take a piece of jewellery from the box, making sure of course that they haven't accidentally picked out their own! I always have the last piece for myself to read, but if you find that it is your own that is left, then get a couple of them to put the jewellery back and mix them and get them to choose again so that no one has their own.

Now hold the piece of jewellery to see, or feel what impressions that you get from it. Like with other modalities you may feel emotions or pains, illnesses or perhaps see images or words may come. Whatever it is, it will be relevant to the person. Sometimes things may be picked up that cannot be verified because of the sensitive nature, that person would not bring up to speak about, so we must just let that be.

There are a lot of mediums and clairvoyants who ask for a piece of jewellery when their client first sits down with them for a reading. This is so that they get the energy link to them straight away. So, you might find that this works well for you to.

THE LOG CABIN

See yourself standing on a country dirt road. The sun is high in the sky and it is gently warming you. You are walking along the dirt road taking in the scenery to the right of you and to the left of you. You will see on your journey that there are fields, some with crops, some vine yards, and some fruit orchards, some with different types of animals grazing or perhaps you may see something different altogether.

You can see that there is a mountain ahead of you as well that the roadway seems to be heading towards. The road dips and curves around. You take notice of the different wildflowers that line the roadway here, taking in the scents and the smells and the grass is thick and lush. There are trees that are dotted along in places as well. There is a gentle breeze that blows, every now and again you feel it as it gently caresses your face and lifts your hair and as it does so you can feel all your cares and worries just drifting away on the breeze. You feel yourself relaxing with each step that you take.

You see up a bit further ahead and you can now see that the roadway does go around the mountain. Before you know it you are starting to go slightly up hill. There is no extra effort on you though walking up hill. The road is still quite wide as you are walking up the mountain side. As you continue to walk you start to see right across the valley either side, all around as the roadway winds right around the mountain.

You continue walking, and further ahead you can see a bit of an alcove. There is a bit of a cutting into this part of the mountain and you can see that there is a grassy expanse here with a pool of water. You walk onto the grass and you sit and look into that pool of water, you just stare into it at your reflection. You allow your stare to just drop, so that you are not really seeing yourself anymore, and you are allowing yourself to just relax deeper and deeper. After a while you will see perhaps some different colours going over your image. You may just see colours or perhaps you will be able to see your true self in all your glory. I will leave you for just half a minute before we continue our journey.

It is now time to get up from looking at your reflection in the pond and continue your journey back up the mountain, back along that roadway. You notice how easy it is to walk up. You look out across at the valley below and farther afield you can see for miles and miles around you. The rock face on some parts of the mountain has got moss and different types of flowers that grow out from it as well. You find it amazing to see how nature will find any little place to put a plant.

You start to get towards the top now where you can see that there is a great expanse of a flat area. When you get to the top you can see that there is a wood cabin with smoke coming out of the chimney.

You walk along the pathway that leads to the front door of this log cabin. Take notice as you have a look at the door, what is it made of, what colour is it? You know that when you step into here this is a sacred space for you, so it is set out and furnished exactly as you would have it. As you open the door and enter somewhere in here you will find the fireplace that has a nice warm fire burning here for you. It has a mantelpiece above it. Have a look around the room, what is on the floor? What is the floor made of? What furniture is in here? What colour are the furnishings? Do you have any windows in here? Are there any ornaments? Is there anything on the walls? I will allow you to explore in here and spend some time, if you have a library of books in here you may want to pick one and sit in the most comfortable chair you can find in here and you may want to read the front cover and then perhaps open a page that feels in the right place to open it and read it and see what it says. I will be back for you in a minute.

If you have been reading a book you can place it back in the library now. Somewhere in this room there is a special gift for you, so I want you to go and find it. It may be on a little side table it may be on the mantel piece or perhaps somewhere else. When you find it have a look at what it is and take it with you. Take another look around inside here, does it have a light source? Are there candles or perhaps a kerosene lamp or normal lights.

And now it is time to leave here. As you walk back through to the front door, you open it and you are outside once more. You stand here for a moment enjoying the view as you have an uninterrupted view no matter where you stand and where you look.

There is a beautiful garden up here near the log cabin. Have a little walk through the garden and you will see that there is a bench seat. Go and sit at the bench seat, knowing that as you do you will be joined by your highest and best guide or another higher being or perhaps somebody that you love that is in the world of spirit. I will allow you to spend some time with them before going on our return journey. Allow yourself at least one to two minutes.

It is now time to thank them for coming and spending some time with you as you get up from the bench seat and walk back through the garden. Walking now down the pathway that leads back onto the roadway, it takes you down the mountain the way you walked up and you notice how relaxed you are as you are walking down the mountain. You seem to be going so much quicker going down than when you came up. You are walking past the looking pond as you are going back down the mountain.

You look up and you can see an eagle high in the sky above you, it is so majestic as you watch it hovering, it has a great width of wing span. You imagine what it feels like to be an eagle as you reach your energy out to it to feel the freedom of gliding along the air currents of the freedom that it feels. You bring your energy back to yourself.

You continue walking and before you know it you are down at the bottom of the mountain walking back along the dirt road where you are watching everything that is going on in the fields. You can see animals grazing, you see some butterflies that are on the flowers that are here and there along the side of the road. You are feeling yourself so warmed by the sun that is above you, and are feeling so nurtured by it. You feel that gentle little wispy wind again just gently lifting away from you all the cares and worries that you don't need to concern yourself with and are just floating away on the breeze. Then with another step you find yourself back in the room very firmly seated in the chair. All the way back now and keeping with you all of the experiences on your journey.

LESSON 7
BLIND READINGS

This is done so that you do not know who you are reading for. This can be especially good for small groups that have been sitting together for a long time and feel that they may be utilising some of their logical brain to access information instead of getting it psychically or from spirit when giving messages to their fellow students.

Place a chair in the corner of the room facing into the corner so that the person in the chair has their back to everyone else. Now, one person is chosen as the speaker. This is so that the person who is being read for has a voice for them, but the reader has no idea in the conscious mind who it is. The speaker points to the person that will be read and they then do the energy connection. The easiest way that has been found to do this is to pretend to dial a telephone to make the connection to the reader.

Now let the reader know that the connection has been made to them. As the reader speaks, look at the person receiving the message for a nod for yes, a shrug of shoulders for I don't know and shake of head side to side for no, etc. The chosen speaker is the only one to talk out loud and let the reader know how they are going with it so that it remains anonymous to stay a "blind reading". Once they have done the required amount of readings, ask them as to who they believed out of the group that they had been reading for and in what order. It is often interesting the information that can be received without us realising who it is for, that we may not have imagined that it would belong to.

Another way to do blind readings is by getting everyone to write their own name on a piece of paper and place it in a plain envelope. The envelopes are then all mixed up together so no one knows which belongs to who. This is interesting as the reader does not open the envelope until after finishing the reading, so they may have even read for themselves! Make sure that you get each one of them to open the envelope as soon as they are done so that the reading is still fresh as sometimes the reader may have to recap on something for the person that they were reading for, and if you wait until the end after everyone has finished doing their reading, important information may have been forgotten and lost.

MEDITATION 7
UNICORN JOURNEY

To begin this meditation either lay flat on your back or sit upright with both feet flat on the floor and both hands resting in your lap. Just allow your eyes to gently close. Take a deep breath through the nose and as you do, imagine that you are breathing in divine golden energy. As you exhale feel all of your cares and worries leave with each out breath.

Now see yourself standing in the middle of a beautiful green grassy meadow with a forest ahead and rolling hills around you.

It's a lovely sunny warm day and the sun is high in the sky, just gently warming your shoulders. There are just tiny little white wisps of clouds in the blue sky.

As you look towards the forest, you see a pathway the leads through the centre of it. You start to walk upon the soft green grass towards the opening of the forest to go onto the path. You notice that it is only marginally cooler in the forest because finger widths of sunlight come through the top of the canopy of the tree tops that form an archway over the pathway. So, you remain at just a comfortable temperature as you walk through the forest.

You take notice of all of the pretty coloured wildflowers in their many different shapes and varieties on your walk. There are different mushrooms and toadstools in a great variety and many types of ferns, including, fish fern, maidenhair, bracken and magnificent tree ferns. As you go further into the forest along the pathway, these plants as well as the trees are bigger and taller, and as you look up, the trees seem to go on forever.

You see a slightly narrower pathway leading off from the main pathway that you have been following that goes to the left. You feel the pull to go in that direction. It isn't too long going down this pathway that you notice the foliage slightly changing.

You can hear a sound in the distance that gets louder and you wonder as to what it is coming along the pathway that is getting closer to you. You are very excited and happy to see that it is a beautiful unicorn standing upon the pathway looking at you. You walk up to stroke it. You can feel that it doesn't feel like a horse's coat, but, feels more like a silken satin in texture.

The unicorn kneels down on the ground and motions with its head for you to climb onto its back. So, you hop onto the unicorn and hold onto its mane. So quiet and quick on its feet, going from a walking pace, to a trot, into a gallop and going faster and faster. You feel so safe, almost magnetised to the unicorn for the duration of the journey. You are travelling so fast that the foliage of the forest is just rushing past you, and you have travelled a great distance in a short space of time. The unicorn begins to slow down as you see the forest open up to reveal a huge pond. There are other unicorns here and they start to walk towards you for a closer encounter. You can feel the love that emanates from these beautiful beings to you.

They all surround you and bow their heads so that the horns are pointing directly at your base chakra. You see it glows red in colour with the unicorns working to clear any dark patches, you see it become a clear red ball of light. Now to the sacral chakra and clearing any darkness here and you see it a brilliant clear orange ball of light. Up to the solar plexus chakra and again you see any darkness dissolving for it to now be a bright yellow orb of energy. Going to the soul light chakra now and it grows in vibrancy as it opens further and clears out debris to become an orb of a peach/apricot colour. Now you see your heart chakra glow with a beautiful rich emerald glowing green light that shines after the unicorns have focused on it. Then the thymus is a beautiful deep rose pink and any dark spots are quickly transmuted making it shine brightly. The throat chakra with its sky blue colour now is cleared so it shines brightly.

You notice that the unicorns seem to be very focused on your third eye chakra that is a deep night sky blue indigo colour. You telepathically receive from them that when your third eye chakra is clear of darkness and blockages and remains balanced, that your intuition will be strong allowing them to communicate with you much easier. They now focus on the crown at the top of your head and the violet orb of colour becomes brighter with bright white light just above it. All of your chakras are now cleared and operate on a higher vibrational frequency level than what they did before. We thank the unicorns for their healing.

One of them comes closer to you now and you feel your third eye connecting with theirs. They have some information that they would like to share with you about your soul's purpose and the sacred contracts that you signed previously to this incarnation. You may want to ask the unicorns for help in your life with your soul purpose for them to guide you to what it is that you need to do or to find the information for. They are only too willing to help if you give them permission. As we have free will, we need to give any higher being permission to help us in any area of our life, otherwise they are not permitted to interfere. Mentally ask this unicorn that you have been communicating with for its name. Hopefully, you will be able to perceive it as you will be able to call upon it whenever you feel the need for its help in creating what you need in order to fulfil your life's purpose. You can also ask them to grant you a wish. If it brings no harm to anyone and it is in accordance with your karma, then they will help you to manifest it. So, spend time in creative visualisation of what you want. (Allow yourself a minute or so to hear what you need to know from them before continuing).

We thank the unicorns again for all of their help. They bow their heads in acknowledgement that it is time for us to leave. Your unicorn bends down for you to hop on for the ride home. So, you once again climb upon its back and place your hands around its neck. You feel so safe and so loved, as the unicorn stands up and turns around. Swiftly and smoothly, going from a walk right through to lightning speed pace. You don't notice the foliage of the forest whirring so fast past you as you feel so changed by this wonderful experience that you are still pondering upon it.

Slowing down again you see the familiar pathway. The unicorn stops and bends down to allow you to get off. Thank your unicorn for all of its help as you turn away and continue to walk down the pathway that will lead you back to where you came through from the meadow. It isn't long before you can see the main pathway that the one you are on leads into. You notice how different you feel walking along the pathway coming back from when you started your journey. So much more relaxed, yet clearer and more energised. You feel that your intuition has strengthened with your encounter with the unicorns and you are feeling so much peace and in touch with nature. Before you realise it, you can see the opening of the forest that leads out onto the green grassy meadow and beyond.

With another step you can feel yourself all the way back in your room. You sit for a minute in contemplation of your experience and keep with you all of the peace, healing, clarity and knowledge gained from the journey. When ready, you can wriggle your finger and toes and allow your eyes to gently open.

LESSON 8

REMOTE VIEWING (WHAT'S IN THE BOX)

Remote viewing is a technique that I consider to be of a more advanced nature, but it is one modality that I get the students to practise on a weekly basis on top of doing whatever is the chosen modality that we are working with for that day.

Mediums and psychics utilise this as a way to find and locate different things such as a missing person whether alive or not, a missing loved pet or just a missing article. So, it is one of the most important modalities that we can hone and develop our skills in, with being of service to help others. Some police forces utilise the specialist skills of some people who are excellent for doing this kind of work.

I have only worked this way once when I was asked some years ago if I could help in locating a missing dog. It wasn't something that I had any practise in, but said that I would give a go to see if I could help.

I got myself into a meditative state and asked for my highest and best guide that could help me to "see" where the dog had gone to. I had already asked the owner for the dog's name so that I could get an energy link to it. What I saw then was what looked like out in the country, and yet I knew that the dog was in suburbia. I could see bush and a dry creek bed, but then all of a sudden I was in a suburban street across on the other side of it. At the time it made no sense to me as how could go from bushland setting straight into a suburban streetscape? The owner replied that there was a reserve parkland nearby and that I did describe the area and that there were indeed houses across from the parkland as

I described. I did not see the house number though where the dog was. So, the lady that was the owner of the dog went door knocking, and sure enough after only a few houses her beautiful little furry companion was there safe and sound! So, don't underestimate what you can do when you need to be able to do it to help someone. I never charged that lady as I said I was happy to help and I wasn't actually that sure whether I could work in that way to find her lost companion. So, I was very happy that they were reunited, the lady had the right direction to search in, as she had said that the dog was old and she never thought that he would have ventured that far away from home!

So, to start off learning this especially for your class students, get a box that no one can see into and place an article into it. Then the students will have to utilise their intuitive skills to know what is in the box. Each week something different is always placed into the box to make sure that it is a different colour, shape, texture etc. Some things are easier than others to pick up their vibrational rate so it is important to really mix it up as to what is in the box.

If you are the teacher of the class and you also wish to participate and you do not have the luxury of someone that is not in the class that can put the item into the box, you can always elect a different person each week to choose what will be in the box and then they obviously do not participate for that week as they sit it out.

I always ask my students to ask for their highest and best clairvoyant/ clairaudient remote viewing guide to show or tell them what is in the box. Depending how the person mainly works is how they will get their message. So, if it is visual, you will see a colour or shape. If it is what they hear from their guide, then they will be told exactly what the item is. Some others will get a texture or smell or perhaps something else that gives them a clue as to what it is. I always say to my students that they get a gold star for any partial hit on a correct guess. This could be just the colour or the shape, smell or whatever can be related to the object.

Like all divinatory modalities practise really does make perfect and the best thing is to not get too hung up on results, but to have a bit of fun with expanding your skills.

CRYSTAL PALACE

Now visualize golden divine white light coming right from source, and into this room, spreading right across the floor, and as it does this a myriad of lights cascade down on it forming now the rainbow bridge. Coming down the rainbow and entering the room now, you see a beautiful Pegasus and it kneels down right in front of you. You know it has come to take you on a journey, so you hop onto its back and you almost feel like you are magnetised to the Pegasus. You feel very secure on your Pegasus as it stands up. It chooses a colour now to step onto and the rainbow is like a conveyor belt going very swiftly though, very smoothly as it lifts you up out of the room.

Pegasus on the rainbow takes you right out, going through the sky on the rainbow, you are looking down at the houses and the cars travelling on the roadways. Very quickly they get smaller as you go further away. Then you look over the landscape, and you can see all the rivers, forests and mountains. You look across at the vast ocean, and you can see the city landscape and suburban crawl. Higher and higher your Pegasus takes you. The colour that you are going up on, that has just come up swirling all around you, is enveloping you. This is the colour for, whatever reason, you most need at this time. Just know that you will absorb in just exactly as much of this colour as you need and no more.

Very quickly now Pegasus has now taken you along the rainbow, going through the wispy little white clouds. You know that you are in a protective bubble around the Pegasus as well. As you go out of the earth's atmosphere, and you are in outer space, you look across at the moon and you seem to be getting closer and closer to it. You go past it, and then you look at all the different planets in our solar system, Mars, Mercury, Venus, Jupiter, Saturn, Uranus, Pluto, Chiron, and the many moons that go around the different planets here, so many stars shining so bright.

You notice how peaceful it is and you can feel the calmness of the energy as you are away from the earth's energy that in comparison is so dense and heavy. You can see that you are heading towards the Milky Way now. The stars are so bright and beautiful. You feel yourself relaxing deeper and further with each part of the journey that you are taking. You are going right through the centre of the Milky Way now.

You see further up ahead there is like this huge tube of white light that the rainbow is heading into. When you enter it on your Pegasus it whooshes and whirs, and you know that it is taking you through a different time and place. When you are out the end you are in a completely different galaxy and solar system. You look across at the different planets and the colours of them and you can see a nebula.

The rainbow is heading towards a bright shining star. It is very hard to see what it is at first. As you get closer Pegasus starts to slow down and you can see it is a beautiful crystal palace. Before you know it you are there, and the rainbow goes up against a beautiful pearlescent roadway. You can hear the sound of your Pegasus's hooves on the pearlescent roadway here that leads up towards the crystal palace, so Pegasus walks up towards the seven steps that lead up into there. Once you are there your Pegasus bows down to the ground again to allow you to easily hop off.

So we count the stairs as we go up them, one, two, three, feeling more lighter and vibrant and freer, four, five, six, you can feel the higher vibrational energy as you are nearly into the crystal palace, seven, all your cares and worries are left behind. You walk into this beautiful crystal palace where everything in here has been carved out of it. All the pillars and columns, the different rooms, everything has been carved out of this beautiful clear crystal, but it refracts every colour that there is. Some rooms may give you the look of one colour and another room a different colour.

Once you to walk past the central chamber that is here, I want you find the corridor. Down this corridor you will see that there are many different coloured doors. I want you to choose the one that feels right. Take your time and when you find the right colour door and then you go in there, you may find that the room may be the same colour, or it may be something different.

Somewhere in this room you will find that there is a healing bed. Now there may already be higher vibrational beings that are also in this room or they may come in after you lay down on the bed. You may find that there are ascended masters as well as Archangels and other angels of light and other higher beings to help you with your healing process. Lay down on the healing bed that is in this room and you can ask for, in your mind, these higher beings exactly what it is that you would like to have healed, whether it is physically, mentally, emotionally or spiritually.

Spiritually it could be helping you to clairvoyantly see, clairaudient, so that you can hear the angelic realm and other higher beings, as well as your highest guides, or perhaps you want you're sensing abilities to be heightened, or your healing abilities to be heightened. Whatever it is I will leave you for a minute to spend some time with these beings. Remember that they are here for your highest good. It is only with your permission that they will do for you whatever is needed. You can also ask them to heal with things that you do not even know need to be healed, anything that you do not need to karmically endure ask them to remove from you. All diseases and disorders that karmically you do not need to have, please remove them and I will be back for you in a minute.

Some of you may feel the sweeping of angel's wings over you as they move away any debris in your auric field from the healing that is being done, and with your permission some of them are placing crystals within you. These beautiful clear crystals so vibrant that if they are placed within your third eye, will give you clarity of sight, your clairaudience will heighten, so that you can hear your highest guide and other beings.

They may be placed in different chakras to help you clear them better. You may find that the beautiful rose pink energy is being placed within your heart now to help heal your emotions. We now thank the higher beings for doing all this healing work on us as you now sit up on the healing bed feeling very relaxed, re-energised and rejuvenated.

As you now get up to walk out of the room, you feel the pull to go towards the end of the corridor where you have not been yet. There is a door that leads to the outside and it goes out into a beautiful garden. The pathways through here are all lined with beautiful flowers and if you have got very good hearing you may hear the songs that the flowers have, these are higher vibrational flowers than what we have on the earth. There are so many beautiful plants here.

Somewhere in this garden you will see that there is a bench seat, so go over and sit on it. You will soon be joined by a loved one that is in spirit if they haven't arrived already, whether they be human or animal or maybe even you're highest and best guide will come to share some time with you. So I will leave you for a minute to spend some time with them before we go on our return journey back.

It is now time to thank whoever it is that came to be with you, as you get up now from your bench seat. You start to walk back through the garden along the pathway to the doorway of the crystal palace. And you walk again down the corridor past the rooms back past the central chamber. You notice that there is another room that has books in it, it is a massive library. I want you to go over and go towards where you are drawn to and place your hands on a book, have a look at the title, what colour is the book? Open it up there may be a word, a sentence, a paragraph you need to read. Now you put the book back as you know you have the words that you needed.

Now it is time to walk back out and you notice that there is an entity that is standing in the doorway, and they have a gift for you, and it is placed within your hands as you begin to leave. We thank the entity for this gift. Take notice of it and keep it with you as we count the seven steps that go back down again. One, two, three, keeping with you all the healing that took place and all the knowledge that you gained, four, five, six, feeling lighter, brighter, energised and reinvigorated, peace and calm and happiness, seven, and you are walking back down hopping back onto your Pegasus again.

Pegasus stands up and takes you along the pearlescent roadway towards the rainbow. You may be on the same colour as you came up on but you may be on a different colour now. As Pegasus goes onto that rainbow that colour comes up to envelope you and this beautiful colour just permeates where you need it, it cocoons you on the journey as very quickly you are swiftly taken now along the rainbow. It is so smooth you don't even feel movement you take one last look around you at this different place.

You can see that tube of white light now as you are entering it and it whooshes and whirs as you go through it. You know that it is bringing you back to the same time and place that you left, as you exit out the other end back into the Milky Way, with all these bright stars all around you.

You can see the earth as a little dot as you look across at the other planets in our solar system. While we are looking at the earth we visualize now Archangel Raphael's emerald green completely permeating the earth to heal her and all the inhabitants. We also ask for the pink ray of unconditional love to also surround the earth.

Then just in front of you a shooting star goes across the sky, so quickly make a wish. You watch as all the planets seem to swiftly go by you as you are going along on the rainbow. You notice how relaxed you are feeling. The earth is getting closer because it is looking so large now and Pegasus very gently begins to slow down as you are now entering the earth's atmosphere going back through the little wispy white clouds. You can now see the earth's landscape, you can see the oceans, the mountains and valleys. Getting closer now and you can start to make out the city scape and the suburban sprawl. All the houses and the cars on the roadways. Pegasus is slowing right down now as you can see the rainbow go into the familiar rooftop that you left. Very gently sliding down now. Now Pegasus just places you very gently and firmly in your chair. You feel yourself all the way back in your physical body, keeping with you all the healing that took place, all the knowledge that you gained, all the gifts that you received. When you are ready, wriggle your fingers and toes and gently open your eyes.

CRYSTAL BALL GAZING (SCRYING)

This is another divinatory modality that I consider to be of an advanced nature. A pure quartz crystal ball is very expensive, especially if you are after a large one. Most people utilise a clear lead crystal ball although some prefer it to be coloured. This is because scrying needs something to use as a focus point. Traditionally, some people have also used a bowl of water as well as some utilise a crystal ball, whilst some others prefer also to use a dark surface of ink placed in a bowl of water too. Any of these methods are perfectly fine to use for scrying. It just comes down to personal preference.

Just make sure that whatever you are using does not have any distracting visuals around it. For example, do not have a brightly coloured and/or patterned table cloth under it, but preferably a completely white or black background. You may want to place a box around it so as to have no distractions from what is on walls, furniture etc.

Get yourself into a meditative state first and then allow yourself to stare at the crystal ball or whatever you have chosen your focal point to be. Once you have been staring at it until your gaze drops onto another level, then that is when you are most likely to get results with starting to see something appear. You may start to see it go cloudy and then it may clear and show you an image. Some people get so good at this that they say it is like seeing a TV screen and watching a movie film unfold before their very eyes.

In a class situation it is probably best to have a few crystal balls so that everyone can get close enough to see into them without having the view of another student in the ball! You may want to use the cheaper option of the clear glass bowl with water for each student. Remember the most important thing is to have something with a focus point on to use to be able to see what you can. You may see things from the past, present or the future.

MEDITATION 9
CRYSTAL CAVE RIVER JOURNEY

Now visualise yourself standing in the middle of a green field. There are rolling hills all around you and you can see that there is a forest ahead and that there is an opening in it. You can see that there is a path that meanders through it. The sun is high in the sky and it is just gently warming your shoulders. You start to walk on the soft green grass. It is a lovely summer's day and you can hear the birds in the forest. You start to walk to enter the forest.

The sunlight still comes down once you enter the forest through the top of the canopy of the trees. Finger lights of sun keep shining through and warming you, even though you can feel it is slightly cooler in the forest it's still just the right temperature for you as you are walking through it. You take notice of the foliage that lines the pathway, all the different coloured mushrooms and toad stools in different sizes. And there are wildflowers in a myriad of different colours, reds, pinks, purples, oranges and blues. Many types of ferns, fish ferns, maidenhair, bracken, and really big tree ferns the further you go into the forest the taller and higher the tree ferns are, as are all the other trees here. As you are going further into the forest now the trees are so tall and broad here and when you look up they seem to go on forever.

You start to hear the sound of water ahead. You can see that there is a river. You look over and see that there are little boats along the embankment. You can tell that the river is not that deep, it is just deep enough so that the bottom of the boat does not rub on rocks that have been all smoothed by the passage of time. The water is crystal clear you can see easily into. You can see all the rocks that have been smoothed and turned into pebbles here.

You go and hop into one of the boats and as you hop into it, you feel yourself very firmly seated in it. You know that you are very safe and secure in it. As it gently and effortlessly takes off now along the river there are many bends and winds along the river and you are out in full sunshine once more. You feel the sun on your face. It is just a beautiful pleasant day. There are lots of birds in the trees and they watch you going by.

With another turn in the river you can see further ahead that there is a big, huge, cavern that is emanating red light that you are heading towards. You are very curious as to why there is red light emanating from this cave that the river just goes right through. It is very bright and as you get closer you can see why. It is encrusted with beautiful rich red crystals, completely around the mouth of the cave. It lines the bottom of the river as well. It is a huge cave, and you are bathed as you enter here in this beautiful red light. You cn feel yourself being reenergised. Know that your whole body and energy system will only absorb in this colour as much as it needs and no more.

You can see now that the red is now becoming an orangey colour. Now it is a brilliant orange all the crystals in this part of the cave are vivid orange and you are bathed in this vivid orange light. Now the orange starts to become yellow and you are in a vibrant bright yellow. This beautiful crystal energy just permeates right through you and each of these colours from the crystals you will only absorb exactly what you need and no more. The yellow now makes way to a limey green and then into a beautiful rich emerald green, like the colour that Archangel Raphael brings with his healing, you may feel your heart chakra respond to this. Now is the right time to release and let go of any emotions that you have been harbouring within the heart. All you need to do is say to yourself, "I now release and let go of all my negative emotions and feelings". As you do this this beautiful emerald green light will replace it.

Then the green goes into a turquoise blue. You are bathed in this beautiful light. Then it goes into the soft sky blues, and here you may feel your throat chakra respond. You may feel your throat chakra clearing now, and then the blues go slowly into deeper and deeper shades of blue until it goes into the deep indigo night sky blue. The crystals sparkle like stars in the night sky so you can still see.

Then the blue starts to make way for a bluey purple colour before you are bathed in a rich vibrant violet hue of purple. This beautiful purple colour is a deepest of amethyst hues. You may feel your crown chakra vibrating and you can see the little boat now is heading towards an embankment where you can see that up on dry land there is a separate cavern that is emitting a very bright white light.

So you step up out of the boat and walk into this bright white light cavern and you can see that what is creating this white light is clear crystals. All these clear quartz crystals completely lining it, the floor of it, the walls, the ceiling it is so bright. In the middle you see that there is a massively, huge clear quartz crystal. It is much bigger than if you tried putting your arms around it you would be almost just standing in a semicircle around it. So if you feel that you can take the vibration of the giant crystal, go up and put your body right up against it and give it a hug.

You may be able to feel the vibrational energy humming though the soles of your feet, as well as your entire body and if you have your face pressed up against it as well and allow this crystal to completely clear your energy fields of all stagnant energy, of all blocked energies, all you need to do is just say to yourself, "I now release any and all blockages and stagnant energy and I absorb into myself all of the higher vibrational clear crystal quartz energy to replace it." You feel your energy shifting. You may notice that you feel a crystal clear clarity in your mind.

There is another part that you didn't see towards the back of this cavern with the beautiful clear quartz crystals. There is a beautiful rose pink quartz just sitting there, it is quite big when you walk up to it. As you do, you put your hands on it or give it a hug, whatever feels right. You can feel that beautiful rose pink unconditional love enter your heart chakra, helping to heal your heart of all past hurts.

Now you stand away from the pink Quartz, at this point if you feel the need to, you can pick up any loose pieces of this beautiful rose quartz, you may place them in your heart chakra or just keep them on you for safe keeping. The same with the clear quartz crystal, if you can find any loose pieces of that you may want to pick them up and take them with you as well. Now it is time for our return journey.

You start to walk out of this bright white light crystal cavern, to walk back out and to go back into your little boat again. Remember that the water here is very shallow, so you can reach down at any point going back and take some of the loose crystals on your way. Once again, you can feel yourself very firmly seated in your boat, if you want to take any of the rich violet crystals now is the time to get them.

As your little boat turns back around and very effortlessly goes back upstream, you notice that you go back up faster than what you came in, so the violet now quickly makes way for the indigo blue. The indigo blue into the sky blue, into a beautiful turquoise and aqua colours, to the rich emerald green into limey greens, vibrant yellow, the rich orange and into the deep reds and you can see daylight now as you exit through the mouth of the cave.

Going back upstream noticing how much lighter and brighter you feel, quite relaxed now on your journey back out. The little boat goes so effortlessly up the stream, going around the twists and turns of the river. The birds in the trees in the forest here, seem to be chattering about you, they have noticed a shift in your energy, they can see you auric field. Before you know it, the little boat pulls up along the embankment where you first started your journey into the crystal cave and you hop out of the boat and you walk back up the embankment where you can see the pathway that leads down into the forest.

You walk down this pathway and feel so much fresher walking down this forest path. You notice that you have more clarity of vision and hearing going through the forest. You can look at something, a plant that is way ahead of you and you know that with your mind that you can just energetically reach out to it and you can feel what the foliage feels like, even though you are not physically touching it. Now you bring your attention back to yourself again as you continue walking along the pathway, you can see flying ahead of you is a pretty little blue bird it seems to be leading you back out of the forest and then before you know you can see the opening of the forest that goes back out into the beautiful green grassy meadow. Once you walk out there you are in full sunshine.

Then the beautiful little blue bird comes and flies along and lands on your shoulder and you know that you have the blue bird of happiness with you. Now with another step you find yourself back in the room, feeling yourself very firmly seated. All the way back, keeping with you all the crystals, healing, all the feelings of peace and tranquillity and the crystal clear clarity.

FLOWER READINGS

This is best to do in spring when there is an enormous choice of beautiful flowers in most people's gardens with which to choose from. Each person picks one flower and places it is a plain brown paper bag to bring into class. All of the bags are either placed in the middle of the floor or placed into a basket, but, done so as no one knows which is whose flower in the bags.

After the meditation get each student to pick up one of the brown paper bags and to look into the one that they have chosen and make sure that they didn't accidentally pick up their own. If this happens, put them all back and do the same again until everyone has a flower that they didn't bring.

Now, pick up the flower and firstly feel the stem of the flower. Does it feel strong and firm or is it floppy and needs you to hold it up? If it is strong, then it shows that the person is feeling strong within themselves, but if it is needing you to hold it up to support the flower, then it is showing that the person is in need of being supported at this time of their life. Are there any leaves along the stem? If so, are they well formed?

Take a look at the colour of the flowers petals as it will tell you about the emotional state of the person. The colour red will depict a person that has a lot of energy and is very passionate, orange shows a person that is optimistic with a happy disposition, Yellow depicts an intellectual person, pink shows a loving and caring disposition. Purple shows someone who holds spirituality or religion very high in their life. Indigo depicts a person with high intuition and blue shows a person who is usually calm and may choose to work in the humanitarian fields. White shows a purity of spirit.

When you look at the underneath of the petals of the flower it will show you about the physical health and general wellbeing of the person. Look for spots and blemishes or anything else that can give you any information. Utilise your intuition to "feel" what the blemishes and spots may be indicating about the person's state of health and any illness or accidents that may have happened in an earlier stage of the person's life.

Now look at the top of the petals as it will show you about the emotional wellbeing of the person. Remember that you will see what is current and what is from the past as well on all parts of the flower. Once again, any blemishes or spots can indicate emotional trauma or heartache including grief and broken relationships.

Right into the centre of the flower will show you about the person's spirituality. Is the flower open or does it hide the centre? When the centre is hidden, it shows that the person is just allowing themselves to develop at a pace that feels safe and comfortable for them. The colours here will also show you the depth of the spirituality too. This is equivalent to looking at a person's crown chakra for their spirituality.

FOREST FAERIES

Now see yourself standing in the middle of a beautiful green field. You see that there is a forest ahead and that there is an opening in it. So you start to walk towards the opening in the forest, it is a nice warm day, and as you enter the forest, where the opening is, you can see that there is a pathway that meanders through it.

At first the forest may seem a little bit fresh, but you still feel warm enough on your walk. It is nice and bright in this forest, as finger lights of sunshine come through the top t of the canopy of the trees, gently warming you. There is lots of beautiful, thick green, luscious foliage here. There are so many different types of ferns, tiny little ferns to huge ones. Some of the varieties are maiden hair, fish fern, bracken, beautiful tree ferns and the further you go into the forest the taller they are. You can see on some of the fronds that there are large green frogs on them and they watch you walking by. There are lots of tiny little colourful birds in this forest. You can see some little rabbits scurrying ahead of you as they see you coming along the forest pathway.

You see that there is a pathway that leads off the main one going to the left. So you walk down it. You can see that there are some beautiful flowers, some of them are very large and some are tiny. You continue walking along here and the foliage gently changes as you are going along this pathway. Every now and again you can hear little noises like there is small little creatures, but you know that you are safe here you are in a sacred forest. There is only good, positive beings that are here.

You feel as if you are being watched, and you walk a bit further and the forest opens up ahead where you see that there is a beautiful field of flowers. Some of them are huge and some are just normal size, some of them are so brightly coloured. Somewhere in the centre of this field of flowers, in the centre you will find that there is an open circle of beautiful soft green grass. So you go and sit in this soft green grass that is in the middle of all these beautiful flowers. And as you walk through the flowers you might be able to pick up some of the scents from them. Some of them are very exquisite, some of them it is a scent that you have never smelt before but very beautiful to the nose.

As you sit here on the soft green grass, you feel quite calm and peaceful. You feel that roots from the soles of your feet go 6 inches below to your earth star chakra. They spin it, and then you grow roots right down to the centre of the heart of mother earth fully grounding you. Then it goes into the highest vibrational crystal kingdom. This is to allow you to draw up earth's vital life force energy and the crystalline higher vibrational energy. You intuitively know that your physical vehicle and your energy fields will only absorb exactly what they need and no more. You can also send from you down into the earth any negative energy that you no longer need from the physical vehicle. This is whether it is negative feelings, negative thoughts, and pain in the physical body or something else. You have a knowing that the earth will completely cleanse it as you are bringing up into you higher vibrational, energised, restorative healing energy.

All the noises that you have been hearing you can see what they are now. There are some beautiful fairy beings, some of them are winged and some are not. They are coming to spend some time with you. You will see that they come with little bags of fairy dust. There are different coloured ones for different things, and they intuitively know exactly what it is that you need for healing. There are some with little bags that they will sprinkle on your third eye to help open your clairvoyance, but only with your permission of course any of this will be done. There are some to open up your clairaudience so you can give them permission or not to do all of this work, but I am certainly giving them permission to do all of this for me. Some of them will sprinkle iridescent dust on the top of your head for your crown chakra to open completely, and it dissolves all blockages and barriers so that your crown chakra energy goes right up directly to your higher self. Also for you to be able to hear, sense, see the higher beings on the higher levels of existence, the beautiful angels, ascended masters and other higher beings.

Other fairies are working on the physical body, including even things that you may not know that you need work on. They intuitively know what imbalances you have in your body and your energy field and they will help you, where allowed, to correct any imbalances so that where you do not need to have illness, or any disease, or disorder, they will alleviate it before it is ever a known condition.

There are some fairies that would like to share some wisdom with you, and some information and you can ask them whatever you like as well. So I will leave you for a minute to share some time with them.

Now some of the fairies are jointly carrying a very large bag of fairy dust for you to take with you. They place it in your lap. We thank the fairies for the gifts of healing on us, what we have experienced, and this bag of fairy dust that you can either use for yourself or if you choose you can share it with others as well to help them with their healing process. Just remember that you have this now so you can use a little bit to help every now and again to expand your clairvoyant vision, or perhaps your connection to source or your higher self, perhaps your clairaudience. Or, to sprinkle on some part of you that is in need of healing, and that area will be cleared and restored. We pick up our bag of fairy dust, thanking all the fairies for all their help.

You turn now to walk back the way you came in, you start walking back through the flowers and as you brush past them you may find that beautiful smells form the flowers come up to you, the most beautiful perfumes. Then you walk back through the forest going down the pathway you notice how much lighter and brighter you feel and any tension on your shoulders that you had is now completely dropping away. With every step that you take you are feeling calmer more balanced and centred, a deeper inner peace. You notice that you have clarity of mind, you have a clear and calm mind and a restored and balanced body and an energetic system.

You see now where the path that you had gone down to meet the forest fairies now joins back onto the main pathway. You follow that back down the way you came in. There is a myriad of beautiful butterflies ahead of you. They are so many different colours, they all seem to be leading you back out from the forest where you can see now the opening that leads out into the green grassy meadow where the butterflies fly off in all different directions. You are stepping out onto the soft green grass again in the meadow, enjoying being in full sunshine, and then with another step you find yourself seated very firmly in your chair. All the way back now keeping with you all the healing. Remember you still have that bag of fairy dust for whenever you need it.

CANDLE WAX READINGS

You will need a candle and a container of water for each person that is in the group. The best candles to utilise for this are the larger pillar style. This is because they have a large top area for more melted wax which is good for doing the readings. I have found that the smaller ones may not offer much wax to work with. Make sure that you can safely have the individual candles sitting in their own container that is half full of water. Light all of the candles so that they are burning whilst the meditation is happening, to ensure that there will be enough wax to do the readings with. You can use any colour candle as it really makes no difference to the reading, you are reading the shapes that are formed. You may want everyone to bring a non-scented candle though, as it could become overwhelming to the senses!

After the meditation, have each of them get their candle and pour the melted wax into the water in the container in whatever way they feel intuitively drawn to do. Once everyone has done this, they then give the container to the person that will read it for them.

Look at the shapes formed by the wax in the water. As always ask for your highest and best clairvoyant/clairaudient guide to help you to read the wax and to give you a message to pass on to the person you are reading for.

As with all things that we look at for messages, this like the tea leaves and other things that form any imagery, you will need to also work with your own symbolic dictionary to understand what the hidden meaning is for the person that you are reading for.

MEDITATION 11
CHAKRA CLEARING WITH GROUNDING

Now see yourself standing on a beautiful sandy beach, and you are watching the ocean waves just gently rolling in. The Ocean is quite calm, the sun is high in the sky and it is just gently warming you. You are feeling very comfortable and relaxed. You are feeling more and more relaxed with each wave that comes rolling in lapping at the shoreline. Just little wispy white clouds in the beautiful blue sky. You can feel the sea breeze gently caressing your face and your hair, and as it does, you are allowing all your worries just to float away on the breeze.

Then from the sun, a golden beam of light comes down and touches your crown chakra. It gently flows through clearing the energy that is in the top of your crown chakra. This beautiful high vibrant colour removes all blockages and obstacles as it works its way through your head, down the chakra column, swirling, moving slowly through it. As it moves through it pushes out the nearest chakra exit, any blockages, any debris.

So it continues to go through, right through the third eye chakra, and for your clairaudience which is right behind the physical ears. So you can imagine there is like a triangle in your head and it clears all of this, pushing out all the debris, clearing it very gently, swirling all the way through and all the related areas of the body too.

It goes right through the head area and comes down right through the chakra column and now into the throat chakra. Pushing out all unspoken words, pushing away and clearing it so that you may now speak your truth easily. This beautiful golden energy now starts to flow down through the chakra column, down through the shoulders.

You will find it swirls at all the major joints in the body too. There are so many chakras in all the points in the body. This golden energy goes right down the arms. You may feel, especially for those of you that do healing, a tingling in your palms as it enters here and pushes out, and down through the fingertips as well. Then it is continues going down the chakra column, going into the thymus now, clearing its way and replacing the energy with this beautiful golden light. It continues to flow through into the heart chakra. This is good for releasing any old emotions of sadness, grief, and any other emotion that is not for your highest good.

You may find too that some of the energy that is being dispersed out from each of the chakras, because it is not for your highest good, is coming out from the backs of the chakras as well as the front.

Then it continues going right through the body as well. It is going down into the solar plexus, and as it is clearing this area you know that it will help your intuitive sensing abilities to be heightened. Now it travels into the sacral chakra and clears this of all stagnant energy too before moving into the base chakra. It clears this area so it glows a lovely red colour. It now moves down the legs and into the knees where it swirls for a while before continuing down the lower legs and into the ankles. It works through and goes into the feet.

You also feel right from the soles of your feet golden roots that go directly down, going six inches below into your earth star chakra, and you spin it until it spins fast and becomes balanced. It sends roots down, and then heads right into the heart of the mother earth. From there into the highest vibrational crystal kingdom. Now you will draw up from the earth vital life force energy for the physical vehicle, and know that you will only absorb the amount of energy that you need at this time. You will also be absorbing the high vibrational crystal energy as well.

You may find for those of you that can see clairvoyantly, that dark energy is being pushed out. You feel all of this beautiful golden energy just absolutely saturating every cell of your being now as it has cleared through the chakra column. You have absorbed as much as you need of the earth's vital life force energy as well.

You stand here looking at the ocean and watching the water just gently lapping at the shoreline, and you feel yourself feeling even more relaxed and calmer with each wave. The wispy wind is still just gently taking away all your cares and worries on the breeze. There is a seagull that has been flying overhead on the airwaves. It comes down to land on the beach, on the sand. It starts digging at the sand with its beak, it has found something and it is motioning towards you as if it is for you. So go over to where it is and see what it is. Now you have your gift or message.

Then with another step you feel yourself very firmly seated back in the room. You feel yourself all the way back, feeling so comfortable and so relaxed so clear, vibrant and full of energy. And whenever you are ready you can open your eyes.

LESSON 12
TRANCE CHANNEL MEDIUMSHIP

As with doing any psychic or spiritual work make sure that prior to starting, that the room you are working in is completely cleared and cleansed before commencing. This is especially important when you are opening your chakras and auric field.

*Please make sure that you have been trained properly to do this before taking your group through this exercise. Each person that is doing this is trusting that you will keep them safe through this entire experience. You as the teacher, must not do trance Mediumship at the same time. This is because you, as the facilitator of the group, are each person's minder.

After the meditation, ask that everyone who is participating in the trance Mediumship, that they now ask for their highest and best trance Mediumship guide to come to be with them and to speak through them for a message for the group.

In your mind ask for your highest and best teaching guide for trance Mediumship to please come and help you with enhancing each person's psychic energy. Now, go and boost up the energy of each person by using your hands as fans by bringing the energy upwards from about their midriff area up past their faces.

Now go to the first person that is going to try to speak, to pass on a message from their guide. You will need to boost the energy again and then lean in close to them and speak softly next to their ear and say "welcome". This is to let the guide know that it is their time to speak.

Prior to doing this for the first time, it is always good to let the students know to at least try to say hello in order to activate their voice box. If the voice box does not get activated, then spirit will not be able to speak through them. It does not matter if they do not perceive any words at this point, but if they speak to say hello, then it will be easier for the spirit guide to talk when they get the feel of working through a physical body.

It is not easy at first, for both the spirit guide and also the student who is the physical vehicle that the spirit works through to do trance Mediumship. The spirit feels the heavy and dense energy of the earth whilst the student feels another being residing within them sharing the same space. So, a small person who has a spirit that when alive may have been a huge man, will feel that they are growing in size! So, it may take a few or several sessions to get any words out besides a "hello".

Once people are seasoned to doing trance Mediumship, they can go on to asking even higher beings by name such as the Archangels and Ascended Masters. A very good friend of mine who actually started out as my student and I had the privilege of training, is named Helen Shilkin and she has a beautiful book out called Healing with the Angels, which contains many pieces of the channelled information from the different Archangels. It is just lovely and well worth having in your book collection.

When the person has finished channelling the message from their guide, ask the guide to now step out of the back of the person. The guide actually steps out of the back of the throat chakra which is located at the back of the neck. You then fan the air from in front of their face towards the back of them to help move the guide out of them. You then need to say to the person that you are going to touch them and then rub the back of the neck with the intention that you are closing off that chakra after the entity has moved out. Then move your hands around the auric field that is around their head in a protective sealing fashion.

This is well worth the effort to keep doing as it enhances each person's psychic abilities with having higher beings speaking through them.

MEDITATION 12
INNER CHILD RECONNECTION

Now visualise a big balloon above your head in your favourite colour, or whatever colour first comes into your mind. See this balloon as expanding, and you can see it seems to be made of a liquid light. It is now dripping onto your head and makes you feel serene and joyful and light and free. As you fill with this energy, you become as light as the balloon, and start to feel yourself float up. You see yourself go over suburbia, above the roof tops and the trees, and you feel so free and full of adventure. You are now going above large expanses of green grassy meadows and farm land. You see a large meadow that is surrounded by a forest and feel drawn to come down into this spot.

You see a large bench seat here and you go over to sit on it. You can sense your inner child is coming to you from out of the forest where they have been playing safely. Take note of what age they are. Do they look happy? They may be sad or angry if they feel that you have been neglecting them. If so, apologise that you have been busy doing adult things and that you are happy to spend time with them now and that you will come back to see them again. Now ask them what they would like to do?

*Remember that you can utilise your imagination, so if they want to ride a unicorn, then one will appear from out of the forest, or anything else that they may ask and want to do. You can ask your child what type of food is their favourite? What is it that they think you – their adult self should be doing to make your life better and happier and more fulfilling? What hobbies would your child like you to learn or perhaps revisit something that you once did that brought you pleasure? Perhaps they want to play a game with you, or perhaps they would like to draw with pencils or use paints to make a picture. Allow your child to express himself/herself. Give yourself time for each of these experiences and do not rush anything.

Give your child a big warm hug and tell them that you love them very much and that you have to go now, but you will come back to see them and spend time with them again. Now give your child a gift. You may be surprised what appears to give as a gift to your child. Your child looks happy and excited with your gift to them. They now in turn give you a gift. Remember this is from a child, so be appreciative of whatever it is that they have given you. It may something very simple, but it has come from your child's heart to yours. Thank them for their beautiful gift. Give them another heart felt hug, and they turn as you say see you again soon. You watch them walk or skip back along the green grassy meadow and back into the sacred forest.

You now feel yourself float back up, and head back exactly the same way that you got to this place to meet with your inner child. You travel high above the tree tops of the forest and feel free and light. You travel very quickly back to where you started, and can now feel yourself back in your room and keep the feeling of being free and light and you can notice a happy feeling and an inner peace as you allow yourself to now gently open your eyes when you are ready to do so.

PHOTO OF LIVE ANIMAL READING

You will find that working with the energy of animals is a bit different to that of a humans. It is always a good modality to learn as it certainly stretches your psychic abilities to work in this way. I personally have a great love for the animal kingdom and enjoy working with them.

Many years ago I went to an animal communication workshop where we spent the day working in a variety of ways to get information from the animals. I have to say I was disappointed because it was only dogs that we got to do the work with and not a variety of species.

We worked with a photo of a live dog, then a photo of a dog in spirit, and we then got to animal communication with a live dog there on the day. We all had to bring a photo of our own furry friend for another student to read. I still got to read another dog! I had brought a photo of one of my cats which the lady was spot on with what she got from him, but she also found the energy of a cat to read was different to a dog's energy. We also did a meditation to reconnect you with your animals that had passed into spirit. To work all day pushing your psychic abilities can certainly give you a headache!

Anyway, make sure that everyone's photos are protected by cling film if they have brought originals as fingerprints on your photos will ruin them with the oils from them. If they have a copy printed from an original that is probably better to work with. Make sure that each student brings a photo of an animal that they know really well as the whole idea is for students to get feedback on what information they get so that they know that they are on the right track.

Start by asking for your highest and best animal communication guide to come to help you read the animal in the photo. Close your eyes and see what pictures come to you, or words that form in your mind. I have found that animals tend to be very visual when communicating what they wish to share with any humans. Some of them though, will share words with you and it can be surprising to some to learn how much animals know and how they feel at times about their life and that of the human companions that they share their life with.

I have found that you will often see an animal's life as a video movie playing where they will show you a scene where they were happy and would like to enjoy that again. Sometimes they will try to get you to tell their human to give them more food treats! Most living beings enjoy food treats and they can't help themselves to the fridge or cupboard like we can, so it is not surprising that you would get these messages from them as they know that this is their chance to be heard!

You may want to have some questions that you can be ready to ask to make the lesson easier for everyone. The obvious one is to ask the animal, "What is your favourite food"? Another is "who is your favourite human"? What do you enjoy doing the most? What is your favourite toy? Is there something that you would like your human to know about? Is there something that you would like to be able to do that you aren't doing at the moment?

You can probably think of more questions than what I have suggested. You will find that some animals will enjoy the chance to share information with you, but occasionally you may get one that will not want to speak. Remember that they are another sentient being and they have a right to communicate or not. You may find if an animal has come from an animal shelter it may be a bit reluctant to communicate due to unfortunate circumstances that it may have endured prior to getting its new loving home. Animals suffer just as we do with a bad lifestyle, which is sad. So, remember to be gentle when asking questions of them as it is with a shared consent that we can communicate with them.

It is really good to get a variety of different species of animals and birds too especially for those of you who would like to get really good at animal communication, or to do it as a career, so ask your students to bring in photos of different types of pets for the others to read.

You can give your students homework too by asking them to "tune into" their furry or feathered friend to see what they get. I once asked my pet cockatiel in my mind and linking into his mind, how many babies were in the nest with him? He showed me one other with him and broken egg shells. I unfortunately have no way to know if what I perceived was correct or not as he was given to me many years ago as a gift.

You can be sure that you will get many people only too happy to allow you to read their pet for free for you to get more practise with animal communication. Like with everything else, practise makes perfect.

DOLPHIN JOURNEY TO THE OCEANIC CRYSTAL VALLEY

Now see yourself standing in the middle of a beautiful green field, rolling hills all around you and there is a forest ahead. You start to walk on the soft green grass towards the opening in the forest. The sun is high in the sky and gently warms you. When you walk into the forest it is a little bit cooler, but you are still being warmed by the finger lights of sunshine that comes through the canopy of the trees. The trees that line the pathway here form an archway overhead.

There are colourful wild flowers and different types of foliage that line the pathway. You notice that it slightly changes as you go through the pathway that meanders through this forest. There are different types of ferns, from fish fern, maiden hair, bracken, beautiful tree ferns, just to mention a few. Some of the plants that are in here look so prehistoric but they are so beautiful.

Some of the leaves are huge and they are shaped so that they are able to hold water. You may notice that some of the frogs in the forest use these as little ponds. They watch you walking by and there are little birds in the trees that you can hear singing their songs. You continue walking through the forest it's a warm summer's day and you can here crickets singing and you start to hear the sound of water.

The forest opens up ahead and you can see that there is a river, pristine and crystal clear. You listen to the way it gurgles over the rocks, and it is so clear that you can see all the different rocks here that have been smoothed with eons of time, with the passage of water going through here. You look further upstream and you can see a waterfall and beyond that there is a bridge. You start walking along the embankment up towards where the waterfall is coming down. You continue walking past that towards the bridge, and you can see that the bridge is crossing over to the other side, to an embankment and you wonder what is on the other side and up over the top. You start to walk across the bridge in full sunshine, it is very warm. You continue walking across to the other side of the bridge and you start to walk up that embankment and the grass starts to become sparse. You can see the soil becoming sandy and you start to smell the sea breeze.

When you get to the top you can see a beautiful beach stretching out before you. It is a large expanse of sand that stretches out before you, and when you step on it, it is so silky soft under foot. The beach seems to go on forever to the right and to the left of you and the ocean is also clear like the river. The waves are rolling in just very gently. So you start to walk along the sand where the sand is wet and firm underneath the feet here. You stand and look for a little while enjoying the feeling of the firm sand underneath your feet. It seems to be massaging them as you wiggle your toes. As you look across over the water you feel so calm and peaceful, and there is a little wispy wind from the ocean caressing your face and your hair, lifting it away from you. You can feel all your cares and your worries floating away on the breeze.

Now you can see a massive pod of dolphins that have come from deep out in the ocean. They are coming in quite quickly. Some of them are doing big back flips out into the air, and jumping back into the water. You know that you can feel that they are coming to be with you. You start to walk into the water now. You can see the sand where it has been lined from the rhythm of the ocean, from the waves.

It is so crystal clear in here, you are waist deep now and the dolphins are coming in quite close. There is a couple that come in, and you go in a bit deeper now to chest deep water, and they flank either side of you and then gently nudge at you. So, you grab the base of the top fin of each of them that are on your right and left side. There are a lot of dolphins in front of you and ahead of you. You know that you can breathe perfectly clearly in this water as the dolphins now take you with them into the water. As you get a little bit further in, the dolphins come over the top of you, underneath you, behind you, a lot more either side of you and in front of you, they form this huge guard of honour all around you. They have taken you in as one of their pod, and so they will care for you as ultimately they would one of their own. They take you on this beautiful journey.

Very soon you are travelling over a beautiful coral reef, there are so many different types of coral here, in different colours, shapes and sizes. You can see a myriad of tiny little fish that live here, they are very brightly coloured. There are some pretty little clown fish, there are angel fish, and there are all different types of tropical fish here. Still they continue taking you further and further into the ocean and it is still so well lit up in here because it is so clear, the sun light filters right down into it.

You start to see ahead brilliant shining lights in the water. They are in big patches, glowing. You are wondering what is creating glowing colour through the water. There are reds and oranges, yellows and greens, pinks and purples, indigo, blue and turquoise, peachy apricot colours and a very bright white light amongst the centre of it. As you get close the dolphins all slow down. Now you can see what is creating all the colours in the water. It is a beautiful clear quartz cluster right in the centre and all around are big clusters of the different types of crystals.

The dolphins intuitively know which type of crystals that you need at this time so they hover you over the one that you need the most. You might find yourself over a beautiful citrine, or perhaps an aquamarine, amethyst, rose quartz, there are so many different ones here. Some of them they may only hover you over for a few seconds before pushing you on over to the next one. They keep bringing you over different types and you feel yourself immediately immersed in the colour.

Know that you will only take in and absorb exactly what you need at this moment in time and no more. So they take you over the different ones, and when they feel that they have taken you over enough of the clusters of crystals you see that the one clear crystal cluster in the centre has a huge terminated point standing in the centre of it. It is very beautiful as it refracts so many different colours from it. They all hold you above the tip of this, with their noses are all around you, holding you. You are laying over the top of it, the point is not touching you as the dolphins are holding you above it.

With your permission, as the can only do it with your permission, the other dolphins are happy, more than happy, to go and pick up some of the loose crystals from these clusters and place them within your auric field, where you need them. All you need to do is say in your mind, "Yes I would like the dolphins to help with my healing process by placing crystals in my auric field for my highest good" and they will go and do it. It could be anything from aquamarine to amethyst to citrine, to lapis lazuli to tiger's eye, smoky quartz. The list is huge because there is so much here. You can ask them for specific things too for healing. Whatever health ailments you may have you can ask them to heal those for you too.

You can also ask for if you want any of your psychic abilities to be expanded and enhanced, including your clairvoyant vision or your clairaudient hearing or maybe your healing abilities. Perhaps help to open your heart chakra, and some help to balance your chakras, strengthen your auric field or perhaps something else. I will leave you for a minute and let the dolphins do their handy work with you and I will be back for you shortly.

You may have noticed that they have picked up some black tourmaline too, to place into your auric field to help protect against any form of psychic attack. Do not be concerned if you see what looks like a dark crystal being placed in your auric field. Now that you have had enough of absorbing in the clear quartz crystal that helps to clear your auric field and all the other crystals, if you gave permission, to be placed within you.

Now they gently move you away from the crystals. The two dolphins that you held the top fins of are now either side of you, and you place your hands again at the base of their top fins and all the other dolphins flank around you once more as they take you back the way they brought you in. You notice how much more relaxed you are and you are just completely relaxing even more now as they are taking you on the return journey home. You notice how different you feel. You feel better, you feel lighter, brighter, clearer, calmer.

They are taking you back over the coral reef now. You can see all the little fish here and it is all so pretty. You can see a big green sea turtle and it looks like it is standing still in the water as you go past with the dolphins going so fast. You notice that some of the dolphins now in the front are breaking away and coming to the back. You notice that you are coming into shallower water. They stop and you are still just immersed underwater now and they all surround you, facing you. Now they release their sonar as one final healing gift to you. Their sonar will break up all stagnant and blocked energy within you, whether physical, mental, emotional or spiritual. They have heard your requests, what it is that you want, so if anyone is blocked with their psychic abilities the dolphins can help with this by releasing their sonar and clearing away all blockages in the physical vehicle and help to breakaway stagnant energy. They free the movement in your body.

They now come up and nuzzle you, and you thank the dolphins for taking you on the journey and for all the healing. As you now walk back out of the ocean you notice that as you are coming out of it you are completely dry. Now you are back on the sand and you turn around facing the ocean again, watching the dolphins swimming back into deeper waters. It is like the ocean is full of dolphins, there are so many of them. Know that you are telepathically linked to these beings now.

You turn around again and you start to walk on the soft sand, retracing your steps back. You can see your foot steps from when you came down. As you go back over the embankment, you go down again and you are walking over the green grass. Then walking across the bridge. You are over the bridge now and walking along the river, going past the waterfall, and you can feel the energy coming off the waterfall, it is refreshing and you feel yourself being invigorated by all the fresh energy. You continue walking along the riverbank until you can see the main pathway that goes through the forest. You start walking back into the forest now. Many of the animals that you see look like they have hardly moved, they look like they have been waiting for you to return.

Those big ancient plants that are holding the water, the frogs still sort of just lounging around in there, little birds in the trees watching you walk by.

You see further ahead that there are butterflies that have been on the wild flowers here. As you get closer they all take off ahead of you. All these different coloured butterflies, with some of them quite large, and they are heading for the sunlight that they can see and the green grassy meadow. The forest now opens up ahead of you. You are walking back again on the soft green grass.

Now you just stand here for a moment on the soft green grass, and there is a golden beam that comes from the sun. It comes down into the crown chakra, this beautiful gentle energy swirls right through the crown chakra, right down through the head area helping to clear and raise the vibrations right through you. Going through your third eye chakra, and behind the ears for your clairaudience, down into the throat chakra, down into the thymus, then down into the heart, swirling down into the soul light chakra, down into the solar plexus chakra, down into the sacral chakra and into the base.

Now it goes all the way down the legs swirling at the knees, then the ankles then into the feet, and six inches below your feet to the earth star chakra, spinning it to its correct vibration. Then golden roots go from that right down to the heart of mother earth. Then spreading into the highest vibrational crystal grid line. Now you also draw up into you the golden light that comes back up from the heart of mother earth, earth's vital life force energy for the body and the highest vibrational crystal energy also now comes up through the earth star chakra. It then goes right up the legs into the base chakra, into the sacral chakra, into the solar plexus, into the soul light chakra, into the heart, the thymus, the throat, the third eye, the crown and right through into the top of the head.

Now you are completely flowing with all these energies. You feel that this has now completely activated you soul light chakra and it brings all your other chakras completely into alignment. It helps to link you also to the central earth sun. And then with another step you find yourself very firmly seated in your chair. You feel very calm, very clear, very uplifted and healed.

LESSON 14
PHOTO OF PERSON IN SPIRIT

Some people can find doing this a very emotional experience especially if the person in the photo hasn't been in spirit for very long. This can be emotional, not just for the person having their photo read, but also for the one perceiving and giving the messages from the photo as they are linked into the energy of that person in the photo, and to the person that they are reading for. You can feel those emotions as if they belong to you and not someone else. With a little practise you will be able to separate yourself from the other people involved whilst still having compassion for them.

As with all photo readings make sure that the photograph is protected if using an original as working with a copy is better for this reason.

Now ask for your highest and best Proof of survival guide to help you to read the person in the photograph. Depending on what your strongest psychic ability is, this will tell you usually how you will perceive the information from your guide. Just like working with all guides for the first few times, it may be a bit challenging as you both learn how to work with each other to get the information through correctly to the recipient. This is why it takes between two to five years for the average person to develop completely as a medium. By working with a variety of skills and modalities you can become a very clairvoyant medium who will be able to see and hear your spirit guides and those in spirit that people are wanting contact with, and also be able to give future probabilities as to what is coming up in the life of the person.

Always remember to be respectful and compassionate when giving messages when working with any modality, but even more so when relating information from those that are their loved ones in the spirit world.

MEDITATION 14
SACRED HEALING GARDEN

Before beginning make sure that you will not be disturbed and are in a quiet place. Either lay flat on your back, or sit upright in a chair with both feet flat on the floor and hands gently resting in your lap with nothing crossed over, as your energy would not flow well for you to get the most out of the experience.

Visualise yourself standing on a dirt country road. It's a beautiful sunny spring day with hardly a cloud in sight in the brilliant blue sky. There is a light breeze that gently caresses your face and hair, and all of your cares and worries just float away on the breeze. The sun just gently warms you as you start to walk along on the dirt road.

You take notice of what is going on in the paddocks on either side of the road. On your journey you may see animals grazing, vineyards, market gardens growing an array of different vegetables, fruit orchards and crops and a national state forest on one side of the roadway.

You have been so busy looking around you that you haven't noticed until now, that there is a gigantic boulder ahead of you blocking your path. You contemplate the best way that feels right to you, for you to get to the other side of the boulder to continue your journey along the roadway. (Take a minute to work out how you will do this before continuing the journey).

Now you are past the boulder, you continue walking. Take notice of the condition of the dirt road, its texture. Is it smooth, is there fine sand, or pebbles, or is your roadway a bit rocky with substantial sized stones? Are they smooth or sharp if there are any rocks?

You notice further ahead that the road ends in a T intersection. Interestingly, directly ahead are huge wrought iron gates that are covered in vines so that you cannot see what is inside. Either side of the gates, you can see as you get closer are tall walls either side that seem to go on as far as the eye can see, to the left and to the right of you. You wonder what is inside beyond these impressive looking estate gates and fence.

As you get closer, your energy magically opens these grand wrought iron gates. You are immediately delighted to see the most beautiful garden inside, and that it is just how you would have planned the layout, the types of flowers, shrubs, trees, the type of terrain – is it tropical or perhaps an English cottage garden, a rain forest, a cactus desert, bushland or perhaps something else or maybe different sections of all of these.

This place is so huge that you may have a great variety of gardens in different areas where manicured gardens lead into a tropical forest that leads into a field of flowers. This is your sacred garden, so it is all of your own making and it is completely safe for you to be in. You can also ask for Archangel Michael to be with you as your body guard and protector if you wish to do so. If you are an animal and/or a bird lover, then you will find very tame and loving furry and/or feathered beings in your garden and they will all be friendly with you.

You continue exploring within your garden, and notice that no matter what the terrain is, that you will find bench seats to sit upon. Somewhere in your garden is a magical healing fountain. I will allow you half a minute to find it in your exploration of the garden.

When you find it, you will see that it is very large. It has a big enough base at the bottom that you are able to lay in it submerged, or you can sit upright in it waist deep. The top of the fountain flows overhead and the blue water cascades over the top of your head and all over you. As you allow the water to flow over you, you realise that it is not water at all, but a liquid blue light energy. You notice that you can breathe perfectly easily when immersed in it. You feel its uplifting energies, and you sense that this is a good time to allow yourself to let go of, and release, anything that you have been holding onto that has been holding you back. All that you need to do, is to simply say to yourself – "I now release and let go of anything and everything that is not for my highest good." Feel any pent up anxieties, worries, negative thoughts, and negative feelings, including anger, resentment, unforgiveness and any other negative emotion just leaving you now. You may notice murky colours going from you and into the blue coloured liquid energy, these are now immediately cleansed and transmuted into positive energy by the healing properties that are contained within the blue healing liquid energy. Your body and energy system take in the healing blue energy to replace where the negative energy had resided within you.

You notice that you feel so much lighter, brighter, rejuvenated and yet also relaxed and calm. You walk out of your healing fountain and continue to explore more of your beautiful lush garden. The air is fresh and clean here, and you fill your lungs with it, feeling it permeate through every cell of your being and completely rejuvenating you.

Somewhere here in your garden you will see, at the end of one of the pathways, a very large greenhouse. When you see it, start walking down the pathway that leads to it. Inside your greenhouse you will find that it is your very own pharmacy – your medicine cabinet. It is filled with a multitude of wondrous things with which to heal us, some things that you can't get from a doctor or a normal chemist. There are pills, potions, lotions, tablets, capsules, balms and bandages, ointments and creams, tinctures and other various things. There are even bottles containing sunshine and happiness and ones of love and forgiveness. There are bandages to put around you for weight reduction for those that need this. There is absolutely everything here that you could ever need, with which to heal yourself, as well as for others. Somewhere in here you will find a basket. When you find it, you can start to fill it with things for yourself and also for others too if you wish. You can use some things straight away whilst putting others in the basket for later. (Allow a minute to gather your goods)

Now that you have your basket filled, it is time to exit out of your greenhouse back down the pathway. You walk back the way that you came in order to return to the main pathway through your garden. You soon see your magical healing fountain in the centre of the pathway and you continue past it. Throughout the garden, you may have noticed bench seats dotted around here and there. Now go and sit on the one that you feel you would like to rest on. You will meet with either your highest and best guide, or an angelic being, an ascended master, or perhaps a loved one that had previously left the earth plane. They will have a message to share with you, and you will be able to ask them questions too about anything that you would wish to. (Take at least one minute to spend time with them before continuing on your return journey).

It is time to thank who ever came to spend time with you and for sharing their wisdom. You now say goodbye, but know that you can come back here again to see them and to speak with them whenever you wish to. You now get up from where you are seated on your bench seat, and make your way back to the main pathway that meanders through your garden. You now go all the way back to the front gates.

You can see the front gates, and as you approach, they magically sense your energy and open before you. You walk out through the front gates and back along the country dirt road. The gates now close behind you after you exit, sensing your energy moving away. As you continue walking along the road you notice how relaxed and calm and yet re-energised that you are feeling. You feel more at peace with yourself and your life as you look around watching everything that is going on in the fields as you walk along the road.

There is an eagle high in the sky with its wings outstretched as it is gliding riding the air currents whilst watching the fields below. You feel as free as the eagle as it soars at great heights. You have been so busy watching what is going on around you, that you didn't notice that your back at the spot where the boulder was on the road at the beginning of your journey, but it is now gone, and nothing is blocking your path ahead.

Continuing on the road you note how much smoother the road is now and it is like someone has cleared the way for you. With another step, you find yourself back in the room and keep with you all of the feelings of peace and calm, healing and clarity of mind and you keep all the goods that you gathered in your sacred healing gardens greenhouse for continued healing on all levels. Allow yourself to gently wriggle fingers and toes as you open your eyes. You may want to write down your experiences in this meditational journey.

How your road was, depicts how you feel you are travelling through life at the moment. A smooth road shows that life is not so challenging for you right now, whilst a rocky road depicts that you are finding your life a bit challenging at present.

How you got to the other side of the boulder shows how you meet and work with the challenges in your life. There are no right or wrong ways to this, as it only shows how you are working through your life issues. If you went to the left, it shows that you are using your intuition, to the right, you are using your logic. If you went over the top, then you do your best to get an all over view of the entire situation. If you went straight through the centre of it, whether you found a door or used some other means to get through the centre, depicts that you aim to get to the heart of the matter for a solution. If you go underneath the boulder it shows that you are seeking to see the under lying circumstances of what is going on.

LESSON 15
PROOF OF SURVIVAL

This is another modality where you need to ask for your highest and best proof of survival guide to give you messages from the loved ones that are in spirit. Getting the information from the person in spirit through the energy connection to the client, is similar to getting the knowledge from working with a photo.

When I ask for my guides to give me information, I always close my eyes as it helps me to concentrate by going inwards to receive the information. Others stare at a space just beside the person that they are reading for, and some will stare into the eyes of the person that they are doing the reading for. You basically just need a concentration point to help you with being able to get the knowledge that you are seeking from your guide and those that are in spirit.

If you see or sense that a person in spirit is standing behind the person you are reading and it is to the left hand side, it will depict a family member on their mother's side of the family. If the spirit is to the right hand side behind the person, then it is depicting that they are from the father's side of the family. If they are to the side of the person, then it shows that they are of a similar age or status to the person, such as a brother/sister, cousin or friend.

As usual be compassionate when giving messages from the clients loved one that is in spirit. Having the connection can sometimes make people very surprised about their own emotions, these may come to the surface, even though they would have thought that they had already dealt with them. Let's face it, when we lose a loved one, we would all just love one more conversation with them, wouldn't we? This is why I always make sure that there is a box of tissues in the room when I am teaching classes or doing a reading or a healing as you don't always know what will come through, nor do you know the other person's reaction to the process.

MEDITATION 15
LOTUS LAKE

Now see yourself standing in the middle of a beautiful green field. You can see that there is a forest ahead, so you start to walk along the soft green grass towards the opening in the forest. You can see that there is a pathway that meanders right through it. It is a lovely spring day, still early in the morning as you are walking into the forest. The air is a little bit fresh but it is still warm, it is the perfect temperature for you to go walking in. In the forest you can tell it is fresh in here from recent rain and you are walking along and seeing the beautiful coloured wild flowers that have recently popped up, and all the ferns, and all the toadstools and mushrooms. There is new growth just everywhere in the forest. There are so many different colours, and so much growth on the trees and all the shrubs. There are little birds that are sitting in the trees, some of them have been busy building nests.

You continue walking, you see a narrower pathway that leads off to the left of the main pathway. You feel drawn to go down this one, so you start walking down it. You notice the foliage, as you are walking in further and further, slightly changes the deeper you go into it. Different types of flowers and shrubs and bushes, and the tree ferns are older here, they are so broad and tall.

Before you know it the forest opens up to reveal a massive big lake with beautiful lotus blossoms on it, in groups here and there over the lake. When you look across the water, some of the lotus flowers are gigantic, they are so huge. There are so many different colours, they are

114

so pretty. Some of them are bright colours, some of them are in very soft pretty pastel colours.

You can see a boat that's right up against the embankment, so you walk over to it and you hop into it. You feel yourself very firmly seated in the boat. Once you are in the boat it effortlessly and very gently pulls away from the bank to take you across the lake. You look down at the water and it is perfectly crystal clear and you can also see a variety of colours. You see that the colours are created by beautiful crystals that are in clusters on the floor of the lake here. You notice that the lotus blossoms that are above these clusters are the same colour and this is why they have grown so massive. Your little boat takes you right across to where the biggest lotus blossoms are.

Now it takes you right up to one of them and pulls right up to it and you see that it is so big, it is like the room of a house. You step off the boat and onto the lotus blossom and it is very firm but yielding as you walk onto it and you go and sit right in the middle of it. You feel so comfortable here, it has a beautiful energy. There is a mist of energy that comes up from the crystals that are in the bottom of the lake. As you are sitting here faeries come around you, pretty little faeries flying around you with little bags of faerie dust. There are different types of faerie dust and different colours and the faeries intuitively know where you need healing. They have different types of healing faerie dust and so they sprinkle different colours here and there. There are all different types of faeries here that help with your healing. They sprinkle the dust in different parts of you. You notice a beautiful iridescent faerie dust that is being sprinkled on your crown chakra, on your third eye, behind your ears, all to help with your clairvoyant and clairaudient abilities and to help you to be able to connect properly to divine source, your higher self and other higher sentient beings. While they are doing this you can actually ask for specific things that you would like to have healed within you. I will just leave you for half a minute to speak with the faeries.

Now collectively, a large group of faeries is holding a very large golden pouch, or sack if you like, with a drawstring on it and it is full of healing faerie dust. They are landing it in your lap. This is a gift for you to take with you. You can use this faerie dust for yourself or to share with others. It is yours, it is your choice. There is one faerie that comes close to you and would like to share some information with you. I will just leave you for a brief time for you to share time with the faerie.

Now it is time to thank the faeries for the gifts and the sharing of information with us. As you stand up from the lotus blossom, taking with you your golden pouch of healing faerie dust. You hop back into the boat. As you feel yourself very firmly seated back in the boat it takes off again. It continues going across to the other side of the lake where you haven't been yet.

As your little boat is heading towards the other side of the lake you see a figure coming out of the forest at that side of the lake. You recognise it as Merlin the Magician, he has a beautiful staff with him. You get to the other side of the lake in your boat. You hop out of the boat as Merlin is walking towards you, and you walk towards Merlin as he greets you. He gives you the staff. Have a look at your staff, what is it made of, what is it adorned with? I will leave you for half a minute to speak with Merlin and he will tell you how to use your staff. There are staffs for many different things and some are made of wood whilst others are made from metal and most have crystals on top as well as sometimes down the length. I will be back for you shortly. We all remember how Moses parted the red sea with his staff that was made from wood and was as tall as he was too.

It is now time to thank Merlin for the gift of the staff and the words of wisdom that he passed on. As you take the staff now and turn to walk back to your boat. As you hop back in the boat you keep with you your staff and your golden pouch of faerie dust. The little boat takes off heading back over the lake again, you feel so comfortable, so relaxed, so healed, so peaceful and yet re-energized. As the little boat goes right across the lake, past all the lotus flowers, going over the different crystals as the colours permeate up through the water. This is such a pretty place to be in. Before you know it you are at the other side of the lake as the boat goes up against the embankment. As you get out of the boat remember to take your staff and golden pouch of faerie dust with you.

As you walk back now, you can see the opening in the forest where you came through. So you walk back through the forest now. Back down the pathway, you continue walking through the forest thinking about all the things that you have just experienced, you seem to be heading out faster than when you came in. As you can see your pathway now re-joins the main pathway as you walk back down it the way you came.

There is a pretty little blue bird that is flying ahead of you, almost like it is leading you back out. You look at how pretty the forest is, the different coloured wild flowers, and before you know it the forest opens up to reveal the green grassy meadow that you started out in. As you walk back into the green grassy meadow you are in full sunshine, and that little blue bird comes and sits on your shoulder and you know that you have the blue bird of happiness with you. That happiness now resides within you.

As you are standing here, a beam of golden divine white light comes from the sun. It touches your crown chakra and gently swirls through it clearing out any blockages, debris, negative energy as it swirls around right through the head area now and goes right through the third eye. It now goes in behind the ears for you clairaudience, completely clearing all this area out of any negative energy and any debris from it exits out the nearest chakra point.

It continues to go down through the head now, and down through the throat chakra and clearing that area out. Travelling down now through the shoulders, going down the arms, right down through the hands clearing out, down the fingertips. Going down now through the top of the chest and at the higher part of the back, and at the same time clearing out the thymus chakra and swirling through the heart chakra.

Also while this golden energy is going right through and completely clearing you, from the soles of your feet see roots going six inches below into your earth star chakra, and then spinning that to its correct vibrational frequency for your highest healing. Then for grounding, send roots from that, right down into the centre of the heart of mother earth, and then in alignment with highest vibrational crystalline grid.

Now as that golden energy comes down through you, simultaneously you are also bringing earths vital life force energy up through you. Note that you will only absorb as much as you energetically need at this time and no more. That beautiful golden energy now goes into the soul light chakra. This is located between the heart and the solar plexus. Then it goes right down into the solar plexus, then down into the sacral, down into the base, going right down through the legs, right down through the feet, going right down the roots and right down into mother earth, linking back up and drawing it back up again.

So, you now feel that the highest vibrational golden divine white light energy as well the highest vibrational earthly energies and your soul light chakra is also linked into the inner sun of the earth.

Now, with another step you find yourself firmly seated back in your chair. You feel yourself all the way back now. Keeping your feelings of being so relaxed, so comfortable and so healed, calm and peaceful, serene and yet re-energised and revitalised and you have with you your golden pouch of healing fairy dust and your staff from Merlin.

INTUITIVE ART INTERPRETATION

This is a very interesting way to read for another person, as it shows you more about someone than you first may think. Believe me, after some practise you will never look at a piece of artwork the same way again!

Firstly, if you are working in a room that normally doesn't have a table up for you to utilise, put up a trestle table. I have a large assortment of different coloured pens and texta colours which the students can use to do their artwork with. I give them each a piece of A4 plain white copier paper to work on and the pens etc are on the table for all to use.

Do not do any artwork until after you have done a meditation as it puts you into an altered state of being, so when you relax with it, you may be surprised what you draw. Nobody needs to be any type of artist to do this as it can be an assortment of scribbles and sketches and doesn't have to make any sense at all.

After the meditation, before you open your eyes ask for your highest and best clairvoyant guide to show you imagery, for you to put down onto paper, to show something about yourself and your future. Now just go for it until you feel it is finished. I sometimes close my eyes again if I am not sure if I need to put something else on the paper. Allow up to 15 minutes for this process.

I get one person at a time to place their art piece in the centre of the table. Then each person takes a turn, one at a time, to say what they believe the piece is depicting for the person who drew it. It doesn't matter if there are several different interpretations, as we all have a lot going on in our lives and all of them are most likely correct in some aspect. This is true, just the same when we are doing other styles of messages to get a variety of messages given to us.

So, when you are interpreting a piece of artwork, take a look at the use of colours and the shapes, styles and squiggles and try and feel also what they are saying to you as the reader. Use your knowledge on symbology to help with this. For those new to working with symbols in messages, it can be a bit challenging and takes time to learn, but to be able to do this, it is well worth the journey. As with all modalities, just be patient with yourself.

MEDITATION 16
TAKING BACK YOUR POWER (SHORT VERSION)

Now, see yourself at the top of golden stairs. You can see that they lead down into a beautifully golden glowing room. You can see all this golden light emanating from it. So we slowly walk down the steps. We count them as we go down, one, two, three, and you feel that with every step you are taking that you are getting lighter, and freer, and more relaxed. Four, five, six, seven, and you enter this golden room.

It is very bright, and your eyes start to become accustomed to the beautiful golden light in here. You know that this a sacred space where you are completely safe. You can call in to be with you if you like, Archangel Michael as your bodyguard and protector and all of your highest and best spirit guides, friends and helpers for the process that is about to begin. You need to choose in your mind a person that you most need to unhook from, cut cords with, and forgive. You may notice that there are a few people jostling for that place, but it will be the one that you see in your mind's eye that will be the one that comes uppermost.

So, I want you to visualize that they are coming in through a doorway on the opposite side of the room. Remember, this is your sacred space, so when they come in they will have to do what you say. So they come in and they just stand there opposite you. Now I want you start to scan over yourself, you don't have to see any of the hooks, just sense or feel that they are there. They might be really tiny, or they might be huge. When you find them, very gently just pull them out. There is a vat of acid that is sitting at the side, I want you to just throw them in there, because hooks are negative and they are not good for anybody. So, I don't want you to give them back to the person as that just means that they can reuse them again on you or somebody else! I want you to scan yourself, take your time going all over yourself. They could be on the front of you, they could be behind you, on top of your head, and they could be anywhere. Just continue taking them out and throwing them into the vat of acid so that they are no more.

You can ask for Archangel Michael and all your highest and best guides, friends and helpers to help you with this task as well. We ask these beautiful beings to continue doing this as we continue to go on with the next step.

Now I want you to reach your hands out towards them, but, not to touch them in order that you can call back your power. I want you, in calling back your power to ask for it first to go through Saint Germain's Violet Flame of Transmutation so it is completely cleansed, and so that only your pure energy, your pure essence now comes from them. This is regardless of whether you have willing or unwillingly given it over to them, it is yours and it not theirs to keep. If they need energy they only need to ask for it from divine source, to fill them. So now, see, sense, and feel your power coming from them through Saint Germain's Violet flame of transmutation right into you. Feel it coming right into you now. You feel the strength just go right through you. You feel your inner strength grow.

If you sense that you may have any of their energy, you now freely give it back. Just their pure energy sending it right through Saint Germain's violet flame of transmutation giving theirs back to them also.

Now that you have done this, I want to visualize the cord that runs between the two of you. It may be wispy thin or it might be very thick, or it may be a heavy chain. You may want to note the colour of it. The darker the look of the cord the more negative the relationship has been between the two of you. Now if you want to reconnect with this person, you can, after disconnecting and cutting the cord, but they must re-do another cord at a much higher vibrational level than what is currently there.

You should be able to find a pair of golden scissors nearby, and then cut the cord with leaving about 3 inches of umbilical cord on yourself. You will find the cord is attached to both of you at your midriff area. Leave 3 inches of it on the other person as well. As you cut the cord, throw the remains into the vat of acid. If you are having difficulty doing this ask please for Archangel Michael and his blue flaming sword to cut the cord that runs between the two of you at both ends, and for him to now throw the excess cord that is left over into the vat of acid. We ask that the cut ends are now healed and sealed and as has been said before if you wish to reconnect on a much higher vibrational level with them you can do so, otherwise you don't need to if you don't want to.

So, now I want you to say to the person, and you may have to fake it until you make it, but say in your mind the words anyway. I now forgive you, for all past hurts and deeds that have been done, as I now understand that it was a learning experience for us both, and I now let you go in love and light. Now see them walking back out of the room out of the same door that they came in. Then the door closes behind them.

You are left once more with just yourself and Archangel Michael and your highest and best guides, friends and helpers in the room. Then, with that, the golden energy from the floor starts to go upwards to spiral around in your energy field. It is going right through your auric field, and as it does this, any negative debris from the process of releasing and letting go, now flies out from your auric field, and this golden energy replaces it. It is spinning right around all of you, it is going faster and faster, clearing you completely of all the debris, all the negativity, from that relationship and that energy has now left you, and in its place is the beautiful golden energy.

We thank Archangel Michael and all of our highest and best spirit guides, friends, and helpers for helping us with the unhooking and taking back of our own power, with cutting of the cords, and releasing us from the other person, as we turn back and walk out of the room. We go to where we walk back up the seven stairs. Slowly, we walk up them, and count the steps as we go. One, two, three, feeling so much freer, lighter, and happier. You can feel an inner happiness starting to grow within your heart. Four, five, six, feeling so much calmer, clearer in your mind, and clearer within your energy fields. Seven, feeling so much calmer and uplifted, and now you are back at the top of the stairs. You notice you are feeling so peaceful, refreshed and relaxed.

LESSON 17
PHOTO OF ANIMAL IN SPIRIT READING

As with the other photo readings I recommend to use a photocopy and not the original photo unless it is wrapped in cling film for protection. So, to start, ask for your highest and best proof of animal survival guide to come and help you get the information about the animal or bird that is in the photograph. You will find that the energy of an animal or bird in the world of spirit feels different to one that is alive on the earth plane. Just trust yourself as to the images and information that you receive with just allowing it to flow. I have often found that the animal will speak words to you, just like a human being would with mind to mind connection.

Read the information on photo reading of a live animal for more details of general readings from photos of our furry and feathered friends.

FINDING YOUR POWER ANIMAL

Imagine yourself standing on a country road with the sun high in the sky. The beautiful brilliant blue sky all around you with white wispy clouds. As you walk along this country dirt road you look at either side at the paddocks that are here. There are some grazing animals, there are some fruit orchards, market gardens, vineyards and more. As you are walking along here on your journey, the air is nice and fresh and crisp and the sun is warm. You are feeling gently warmed. It is a nice morning walk you are going on. You can see further ahead beyond all the farming fields, there is a forest right up towards the right in the distance. You can see it is surrounded by mountains, you know when you get to the right place because there is a walking track and there is a sign on the right hand side of the road.

The sign reads Sacred Quest, and there is a pathway that leads into the forest here. When you walk into the forest it feels almost magical. There is quite an enchanted feeling in here. You continue walking along and you take notice of all the foliage that is in here because it is changing as you are going through. Everything is so lush and green. You hear in the distance the sound of a waterfall that is going into a river. You continue to walk and you notice bit by bit, that you are walking down and around and you can see a valley below that you are heading towards. You continue walking around and down the side of a bit of a hilly slope that goes down the side of a mountain and lined with beautiful tree ferns and fish ferns, there is even greenery where there is a bit of a rock face. You can see green moss on it. And somehow there are some colourful small flowers that are also around the moss on this rock face. You continue walking and you can see down to the forest floor in parts and you look at the massive trees that are in here. As you are getting closer and you continue walking down you can see that this is a very ancient part of the world this forest. It is a beautiful place for you to go into and it is completely safe for you to be in.

You continue walking, and before you know it you are going down to the last little bit to walk in to the forest that is down here in this valley. It is nestled between surrounding mountains and you walk through this pathway knowing that somewhere in here you are very shortly going to meet your power animal. You feel excited. You are wondering what type of animal or perhaps it is a bird that you are going to meet with.

Somewhere nearby, there is a central clearing and you will find a meeting place where there should be a bench seat for you to sit on. If your power animal hasn't already come up to meet and greet you, it is now coming up on the opposite side of the path to greet you. So sit on the bench seat and be with your animal. You should find that there is a bowl of water for it and the kind of food that it likes to eat, so offer it some. Your animal will mentally, telepathically communicate with you. You can ask it if there is anything that it needs from you. You can ask it is there any special messages that it has for you. You can ask it, what its role in your life is. I will leave you for a minute to spend some time with this beautiful being before we continue...........

And now from another part in the forest comes one of your beautiful animals, that had previously been with you, but has passed into spirit, has now come to be with you also. So, they come to be with you now, you see them as vibrant and healthy and you know that they are happy, and you know that they are happy spending time with you now. You know that you can mentally, telepathically communicate with your beautiful little friend. Allow yourself a minute to spend some time with them.

And now it is time for your beautiful little friend that is in spirit to go back down the pathway, back to the realm where they belong. Now your power animal stays with you and walks back out with you along the pathway that led you into this forest, this beautiful enchanted forest.

So you now walk out of the forest along this pathway and you notice that there are some beautiful plants that you have never seen before. You take notice of them, and continue walking, and now you are at the edge of the valley to start to walk along the pathway back up and around the mountain. Then your power animal says that it will wait for you here and that it will be here for you whenever the need arises and that they are never far away just a mere thought or feeling. They know when they are needed. And we thank them for spending time with us, and they watch us walk back up the pathway.

The pathway goes around the mountain and it is an effortless walk. It feels like we don't even notice the incline, and we feel quite joyous with having had the connection with our beautiful power animal. And also the reconnection with our beloved pet, although that connection was never lost between you and your loved pet that is in spirit. You are pondering about all of that as you continue walking.

You can hear the waterfall, and you feel so relaxed hearing the sound of rushing water. You are breathing in the beautiful fresh air, and even the air seems different here in this beautiful sacred part of the world.

Before you know it, you are up and out of the valley walking back along the walking track. You look around and take notice of the beauty that surrounds you and look at the little birds that fill this forest, and then you are walking back out to the country dirt road. You are going back the way you came, and looking out across at everything that is going on upon the land either side of the road. You look up and you can see an eagle high in the sky, just hovering. It seems to be watching over you. You continue walking and you feel so much at peace, so tranquil, so at one with everything. And then with another step you find yourself back in the room very firmly seated in your chair. Feeling yourself all the way back now.

MEDITATION 18

ZEN GARDEN

Visualise yourself standing out the front of beautiful entry pillars, these stand either side of an opening that leads to a pathway to a meditational garden with a golden temple. Each side of the pathway you can see pretty pink cherry blossom trees in full bloom. As you enter the garden you can see that there is a red bridge that goes over a beautiful lake. You start to go towards the bridge. There is a garden along this side of the lake that has sand swept in a pattern with white stones and boulders selectively placed and you stand here in contemplation. (Allow a minute)

As you reach the bridge and start to walk on it you notice that the pond is filled with bright orange/gold and white/silver coloured koi fish. There are lotus and lily flowers in a myriad of different colours and sizes. It is so peaceful here in this lovely garden no matter where you walk through it. You watch the koi fish swimming around the flowers and some of them are taking extra notice of you and come closer. You look into the eyes of one of them and notice that you seem to be able to hear their thoughts. These are wise and old fish. Stay for half a minute to share your thoughts with them through mental telepathy.

You now continue walking along making your way to the golden temple, as you do you admire the manicured gardens along your journey. You see bonsai trees in one part of the garden that would be many centuries old. This golden temple has beautiful adornments in it and has an array of flowers at the worshipping altar. You can smell the incense in the air that is mingled with the scent of the flowers. You sit here now in a meditative state. A higher being comes in to spend some time with you and to speak with you. (Allow a minute before continuing).

A gift has been placed in your hand for you to take with you, from the higher being that had come to spend time with you. Getting up to leave the temple you begin to walk back out to go along the pathway that leads back to the entrance. You feel very peaceful as you continue to walk through the garden enjoying, taking in the fresh scent of the cherry blossoms as you go back out the gateway.

With another step you find yourself back in your room and you keep the peace and serenity that you attained through the meditation. Slowly open your eyes as you wriggle your fingers and toes.

MEDITATION 19
RIVER OF FORGIVENESS

See yourself standing on a country dirt road. The sun is high in the sky and it is gently warming you. You are walking along taking in the surroundings. You see up further to the left that there is a forest. You are looking at all the wildflowers that are lining the country dirt road. You are looking over and seeing what's happening in the fields. You can see that there is a gateway in the fence that leads into the forest. You open up the gate and then close it behind you. You walk across the soft green grass. You can see where there is a pathway that meanders through the forest here.

The trees are very tall and broad as you continue walking as you enter through under the archway that is overhead made by the trees either side of the pathway through the forest. There is dappled sunlight that comes through and you hear the occasional bird in the trees and you can also hear the gentle tinkling sound of water. As you get a little further ahead there is little bit of a green expanse and you can see the river and there is a huge boat, it is a beautiful looking boat sitting on the river.

The river is only just wide enough to take this boat and just deep enough as well. You walk over to the boat to hop into it. You will find that where you are sitting that there is a big black texta pen there, and you can see all these white boxes, and you know that they are for you to write on all the things that you need to let go of and forgive. The boat just effortlessly takes off.

You enjoy the sunshine radiating upon you, and you look up to see the blue sky with little white wispy clouds. There is beautiful foliage that lines the river banks you feel quite calm and peaceful on this journey. You start picking up the boxes to write on them. These are all the things that you need to let go of. Some boxes are small and some are large, you may find that as you are writing on them they expand. You know that you are pouring into them all those negative feelings and thoughts and thought patterns and emotions. You may want to put on them words like un-forgiveness and when you have done that you throw it into the river and it will disappear in it. This is the river of forgiveness and when you write on your boxes and throw them into this river, the situations and emotions will be worked through and gone. So keep going with other words like resentment, anger, frustration, fear, loneliness, aloneness, bitterness, jealousy, envy and any other word that you can think of.

You also may want to start to pick up different boxes, one for each person, and write the name of the person that you know has wronged you in some way, whether it be words or deeds, so that you can release yourself from all of this. Everyone lets us down at times, even the people that we are closest to, and you may be writing their names first then throwing those boxes into the river. Also situations that you feel that you need to write quite a bit about on a box to then throw into the river. I am going to leave you for a minute to give you time, so that you can have a look and see what it is that you need to let go of and trust yourself with what comes up. If you get stuck at any point you can call on your highest and best guide to come and be with you, and help you with this exercise. I will be back with you shortly.

Now remember to make sure you write your own name on one of the boxes as well and throw that into the river, because each of us, to ourselves, is the most important one to forgive, for any wrong doings that we have ever done, or anything else that we need forgiveness for.

Then, before you know it, the boat has come full circle and is coming back to the place where you started. It just goes up to the river bank again. Before you get out of the boat you will find a rainbow coloured box and it has a gift for you inside. You can also keep the box if you want as it contains all the colours that there is. The box is very beautiful and now open the box and see what is inside. If it is appropriate you can place it within your heart chakra otherwise you can just carry it with you.

Now hop out of the boat and walk back on the soft green grass. Notice how much freer you feel, you feel so much more relaxed and peaceful with every step that you are taking. As you realise that you have released things that you were carrying and holding on to that you didn't need to and they are gone now in the river of forgiveness.

You enter the forest again, walking back through. Now, besides feeling relaxed and peaceful, you are feeling a new vibrant energy coming up through you, and you feel that you are now able to take on new challenges in your life, positive things, those things that you have been putting off doing, those things you have put on the back burner, different ideas that you have had, inspiration that you had at one point, remember those things and bring them into your life now.

Now you are out of the forest and walking in the green grassy meadow, and heading towards the farm gate where you had entered. Once you are there, open the gate and then close it behind you. Then walk along the dirt road again enjoying the sunshine. Continue walking along the road, looking around at what is going on in the surrounding paddocks. Then with another step you find yourself very firmly back in the room now, and firmly seated, keeping with you the gift, and all the positive things that you gained.

ABOUT THE AUTHOR

Karen Bernabo started her journey with the spiritual world from when she was born. Karen recalls being able to see and hear spirit as clearly as seeing and hearing a person that is in a physical body and not being able to tell the difference! That ability was lost when she was still a small child through her gift being misunderstood, but was still left with a heightened intuitive ability. In her teens she experienced premonition dreams and astral travelling. It was with the death of her first love that she began to see spirit again with him visiting her that led her to go to spiritualist churches to seek out spirit mediums for answers.

Karen Bernabo began training in 1995 under the guidance of a Spiritualist minister with the International Council of Spiritualists to regain what she once had with attending weekly Psychic Development/Mediumship classes for the following seven and a half years. In this class Karen learned mental Mediumship, trance Mediumship, tea leaf reading, psychometry, oracle card reading, flower readings, drawing readings, blind readings to name just a few. Because of this it gave her the skills to be able to teach all that she had learned.

Karen is registered to teach under the International Council of Spiritualists and is registered as Rainbow Bridge Spiritual Healing Sanctuary.

Karen also learned Spirit Healing, Angelic healing and Spiritual healing, Crystal healing, Colour and Sound therapy healing, Numerology, Intuitive Tarot reading that were all at least 10 to 18 week courses in length.

Karen also learned Chakra Balancing with the Horstman Technique. Then in 2002 became a Reiki/Seichem Master. Serenity Vibrational healing level 1 was next in the learning experience of modalities and in 2013 Karen learned Shamballa 1024 Reiki levels 1, 2, 3 and Masters which was a life changing experience and a wonderful healing modality to share with others as quite a few steps up vibrationally from being a Reiki Master.

Karen currently resides in the Yarra Valley with her husband Frank and a menagerie of animals including her personal breeding cattery of Birman cats and Maine Coon cats, along with cockatiels, lorikeets and a Shetland sheepdog that loves to try and round up our pet alpacas.

Karen can currently be found running her shop that has gift ware, a vegetarian café with a teaching and healing centre called The Mystics Secret, which is located at 22 Collins Place, Kilsyth, Victoria, Australia, 3137. Phone (03)9723 9955. Follow us on Facebook for updates as to what we have coming up at the shop. Email: shamanbirmans@msn.com www.themysticssecret.com

Karen is currently running weekly psychic development/ Mediumship classes, also 10 week course in Intuitive Tarot, Reiki/ Seichem levels 1, 2 & Masters that include learning Angelic healings, Spirit healing, Spiritual healing, chakra balancing and clearing, cleansing and protecting yourself, room and house clearings and cleansings. Also Shamballa 1024 Reiki levels 1, 2, 3, and Masters, Crystal healing with colour and sound healing 6 week course, Ear candling 2 hour workshops, and Psychic tea parties for 4 or more. Karen is also available for personal sessions of Clairvoyant Tarot with tea leaf readings, Angelic Reiki/Seichem spiritual healings, Past Life Regressions, Crystal healings and ear candlings and creative classes and workshops.

Karen has one audio CD on Psychic protection available through the shop that is a repeat after me step by step guide for self-protection and for the home plus more.

Guided Visualisation Meditation audio CD's are to come later in 2015and early 2016.

Other books due to be released that Karen Bernabo has authored later in 2015:

Past Life Memories: Karma and Reincarnation
Due to be released early 2016:
Archangel Raphael: Angelic Reiki with Spirit healing

Recommended reading:

Anything by Louise L Hay all of her books as well all of her audios.
Publisher Hay House

Anything by Doreen Virtue both books as well as her audios. Publisher
Hay House

Angelic Healings for the Heart written by Helen Shilkin & photography
by Peter Kerverec Publisher Balboa Press

Printed in the United States
By Bookmasters